HARDCORE ZEN STRIKES AGAIN

HARDCORE ZEN STRIKES AGAIN

BRAD WARNER

COOPERATIVE PRESS
CLEVELAND, OH

Library of Congress Control Number: 2012938014
ISBN: 13978-1-937513-07-8
Published by Cooperative Press
http://www.cooperativepress.com

Every effort has been made to ensure that all the information in this book is accurate at the time of publication, however Cooperative Press neither endorses nor guarantees the content of external links referenced in this book.

If you have questions or comments about this book, or need information about licensing, custom editions, special sales, or academic/corporate purchases, please contact Cooperative Press: info@cooperativepress.com or 13000 Athens Ave C288, Lakewood, OH 44107 USA

FOR COOPERATIVE PRESS

Senior Editor: Shannon Okey
Assistant Editor: Elizabeth Green Musselman

TABLE OF CONTENTS

INTRODUCTION TO THE BOOK

There are two main reasons I chose to title this collection *Hardcore Zen Strikes Again*. The first is probably obvious. *Hardcore Zen: Punk Rock Monster Movies and the Truth About Reality* has been my best selling book so far. Marketing this one as its sequel can't possibly hurt sales.

The other reason I used that title is because this really is the book *Hardcore Zen* striking again. The essays contained herein formed the backbone of what became the book *Hardcore Zen*. Most of these pieces appeared on a website I created in 2001 called *Sit Down and Shut Up*. Once a week I would put up a new article about my life as a Zen Buddhist monk and practitioner, what the philosophy meant to me and what I hoped others might get out of it.

The website was far more popular than I ever imagined it would be. At the time I thought maybe a few of my friends might read it. I never really expected anyone I didn't know to even find it, let alone follow it. But within the first few months my inbox was filling up with emails both praising the site and emails telling me that I was a blatant phony who was doing untold harm to Buddhism. I was, in short, a success.

The first essay in this collection is titled "Zen is Punk, Punk is Zen." At the time I wrote it I was starting to rediscover my punk rock roots. I'd been part of the hardcore punk scene in Ohio some twenty years earlier. But by the mid-eighties I was bored and disgusted with punk. My early heroes had mostly either given up or sold out and the once cutting-edge scene had turned into little more than an excuse for the brain-dead louts we once opposed to get wasted and beat people up. I was over it.

Then something unexpected happened. Punk rock came to life again. Maybe it had never really died, just burrowed even deeper underground. I started following some of the then-current punk scene and began to reflect upon how deeply connected my punk rock life was to my own take on Zen Buddhist philosophy and practice. I became convinced that Zen was far more authentically punk rock than most punk rock could ever hope to be.

The second essay, "Zen is not Punk," speaks about how I might have been wrong about this. But then again, Zen is at its core a philosophy of deliberate contradictions.

I find some of my early writings highly uncomfortable to read. And yet I can't repudiate them. I was being honest. I can't even say that what I write now is objectively better than what I wrote then. In terms of style and technique what I write these days is certainly clearer and less self-conscious. It also comes from a different place. I'm happier now and a little less frantic. But the angrier and more frenetic person I was a decade or more ago also deserves to be heard.

Many of these essays were reworked and became chapters of *Hardcore Zen*. Josh Bartok, my editor at Wisdom Publications, worked hard to make my spiky and often deliberately off-putting prose into something that might have a chance at being accepted. He did a good job. The book still sells well, though not nearly well enough for me to make a living off of it. But I didn't get into Buddhism or writing books to get rich. I got into both because I was searching for something deeper and truer than what the mainstream offered.

The term "hardcore zen" is often a source of great consternation and confusion to people who first encounter my work. When I give lectures all over the world, there are many times when I find myself billed as a teacher of something called "hardcore zen," as if it's a new brand of zen. Others who encounter my work some-times assume that "hardcore zen" implies I teach a more radical, more "hardcore" form of zen than they might find elsewhere. They imagine that I'm trying to disparage other zen teachers and institutions by contrasting my hardcore form of zen with less hardcore forms of the practice.

This leads certain people to read absolutely everything I write in terms of an imagined "my religion can beat up yours" attitude that they believe I espouse. And looking back on some of the early writing of mine I've included in this collection it's hard to blame them. It really does sound like I'm saying that sometimes, even to me. But I have the advantage of knowing that I never felt that way. Whenever it sounds like that what I'm really trying to do is to get myself and perhaps those who read my work to take things a step or two further than they might be comfortable with. I think this is an essential part of Zen practice. Whenever you think you've got it, you clearly do not and you need to go another step out of your comfort zone.

Actually the phrase "hardcore zen" wasn't an attempt by me to show how much tougher I was than anyone else. In fact I didn't make up that phrase at all. It was invented by someone in the marketing division of Wisdom Publications after they rejected the original title I gave to my first book. I'd titled that book *Sit Down and Shut Up*, which I thought of as a nice way to encapsulate what it is we do in zen practice. We sit down and we shut up. The phrase also sounded sufficiently "punk," which was appropriate since the book was about how my association with punk rock led me to Zen practice.

The folks at Wisdom worried that the title sounded too negative and would alienate readers. I believe it was my editor, Josh Bartok, who suggested *Hardcore Zen* as the title. The particular branch of punk rock I'd been involved with was called "hardcore punk," so the title made sense and sounded very cool. It also sounded a lot like the title of another book that was then unpublished but which already had a lot of hype surrounding it, *Dharma Punx* by Noah Levine. Josh was aware of that book. I was not. The title *Hardcore Zen* could be expected to attract the same audience as *Dharma Punx* and that couldn't hurt since *Dharma Punx* was expected to sell by the truckload.

I'm not trying to imply that the name Hardcore Zen was forced upon me. I liked the title *Hardcore Zen* a lot and have continued to use it in various ways ever since. It's just that I often have to explain what it means. Which is fine.

I've added new introductions and afterwords to each of the essays included in this book. On the one hand I did this so that those who've already read these pieces for free on the Internet wouldn't feel ripped off at having to pay for them. On the other hand I also did it to try to give interested readers some idea where my journey had taken me in the years since I wrote this stuff. Like I said earlier, these introductions and afterwords aren't meant to be taken as corrections to or apologies for the things my younger self said. They're just offering a different perspective and maybe a slightly better phrased explanation of what I think now that I was trying to say back then. But really, I'm not that person anymore. So I have to let him speak for himself.

I've resisted rewriting these essays. For one thing, I'm too damned lazy to do that. But for another, I've always hated when artists tampered with their own earlier work. I have no interest in seeing George Lucas' "improved" versions of the Star Wars films. I like seeing the wires holding up the model spaceships! I like seeing the puppet version of Yoda! It gives the movies a human-ity the newer versions don't have. I'm just as embarrassed by my younger self's failings as Lucas is. But I don't think it helps to hide them or second-guess them. I've made a couple of small corrections here and there. But for the most part these essays are exactly as they were when I first unleashed them upon an unsuspecting world.

I hope you enjoy them, even if they sometimes make me cringe.

CHAPTER 1

PUNK IS ZEN, ZEN IS PUNK

INTRODUCTION

This is not the first piece of Buddhist inspired writing I posted on the Internet. The piece itself says something about my Zen-themed webpage having existed for less than a month. I'd assume, then, that this must be around the third thing I put up there. I used to try to post once a week. The reference to bin Laden dates it as sometime after September 11, 2001. My guess is it must have been a two or three weeks after.

Here's what I can remember about my early career as a Buddhist blogger. For one thing, if the term "blogger" was in general use at the time, I wasn't aware of it. I had a certain amount of free webpage space as part of the Internet package I'd signed up for in 1996 or '97. For a while, I used this space to host a webpage dedicated to a fictional low budget science fiction movie director named Ben I. Goldman. I was writing a novel about Goldman's exploits and the webpage was intended to promote it. That novel, *Gill Women of the Prehistoric Planet*, is at long last set to be published this year (2012) by Elay Books.

Sometime in 2001 I got tired of the Ben I. Goldman site and decided to try something new.

Parts of this article appeared in my first book *Hardcore Zen* in a somewhat different form. It's a lot more aggressive sounding than anything I'd write today.

THE ARTICLE

The Truth doesn't fuck around. It doesn't care about your opinions. It doesn't care if you don't believe in it. It doesn't give two shits what religion you are, what country you're from, what color your skin is, how rich or poor you are. None of what concerns you concerns it in the least. It is not open to negotiation. You either go along with it, or it will sweep you aside.

Once you do open up to it there is nothing you cannot do. Life becomes so incredibly joyful you cannot help but smile even in the face of unimaginable tragedy. Even the pain you face in your life becomes a source of joy. This joy is not happiness. This joy makes the giddiest happiness you've ever felt look like the worthless waste of time and energy it was. It's the kind of joy that makes every single moment of your life, from waiting around to have a tooth drilled, to sweeping up the basement, to making dinner or looking around for a really nice pair of shoes, so utterly and incomprehensibly wonderful you can't imagine what your life must have been like without such joy.

Good for you, I've heard you say, so you've found the Truth. The rest of us haven't and will not so why should we listen to you? You sound like a clown, Brad. What you're saying isn't the least bit constructive. Look around! For God's sake World War III is about to get under way and you're telling us to be happy about it?! Go fuck yourself Brad. I'm gonna turn on CNN and get the real truth!

You want to know what's gotten us into this mess? We are living in the fucking Garden of Eden and all we can do is bitch and complain—try to find something better. This world is better than Paradise. Why? Because we can never live in Paradise. But we are living right here. Wake up! The solutions proposed by our political leaders, our religious pundits, the guy next door, the talking heads on TV, the warmongers, the peaceniks, the left wing, the right wing, all those solutions are worthless. Confusion will only lead to more confusion. Ambition, whether it's directed at being a martyr for some twisted version of Islam or at being the Greatest Peace Maker of Our Times is just ambition. It won't solve a God damned thing.

This page has existed less than a month. I estimate its readership somewhere less than ten but slightly over five. And already people are criticizing my approach. This page is obviously not Zen because we know what Zen should look like and this isn't it.

Hey, maybe you should turn on your TV. Look at bin Laden. If that guy isn't the very image of what a Holy Man should be, I don't know who is! He's got the little beard, the clothes (any man who wears a dress has just got to be Holy as Shit), the even measured way of speaking. He makes the Dalai Lama, Sai Baba, Ram Dass, the Pope and any self-styled Zen dude I've ever encountered look like rank amateurs. No wonder so many people love the guy and are willing to give up their lives to serve his vision of a New and Better Tomorrow. You want to know what your version of Zen looks like? There he is. Go ahead and chant your Heart Sutras all over him. Forgive me if I do not join in. Religion is what got us into this mess and I want no part of it.

Why all the hostility, Brad? A strange compensatory reaction to self doubt? Your version of Zen sounds like a lot of horse shit, Brad. A lot of anger and resentment and yelling. Where's all that Inner Peace and Calm that we know Zen is supposed to be about?

Zen is punk. Punk is Zen.

Zen has been picked up by Western culture then set aside several times. First the scholars noticed it as a fun and fascinating new religion they could study. A little while later groups like the

15

Theosophists got into the mystical aspects of Tibetan Buddhism and paid a bit of lip service to Zen. I think they liked the temples. In the 50s, the Beats picked up some of DT Suzuki's books and figured they'd found The Answer. Though they couldn't comprehend a word of what they read (and it's no wonder, I doubt DT Suzuki understood a word of what he wrote!), they were quick to espouse the philosophy and clog up the book stores with their interpretations. I think they liked the black clothes. The hippies had no use for Zen. Too bland and colorless. Let's all chant Hare Krishna and eat vegetable samosas, dude!

Back in the late 1970s, I was a teenage musician. Rock and roll was my life, but everything they played on the radio was crap. Not just some of it, but for a while every single piece of rock music you heard on the radio was worthless. Punk rock turned my little head around and gave me a reason to live. When punk turned turgid and conservative in the mid-80s I gave it up. But punk managed to somehow come back to its roots and become a major force again in the 1990s. There's still a lot of conservative garbage out there. But it's the attitude I admire.

Buddha's last words to his followers were "Be lights unto yourselves." Do you understand what that means? Question authority. Question society. But take it all the way. Question punk authority. Question punk society. Question your own rules and values. Question Zen society. Question Zen authority. Go right up into your teacher's face and ask him for the real answers. If he rings that little bell to tell you time's up, walk right out and never look back. No matter what authority you submit to, whether it's bin Laden or George W. Bush or Jesus H. Christ or Dogen Zenji himself, that authority is wrong. Authority is a coward's way of deferring responsibility for his own actions. Tear it down! Kick it in the ass and tell it to get the Hell out of your way.

Punk is Zen, Zen is Punk

As a true punk, my credo is, in the words of the late Ig Nition of the fabulous F-Models, "what your opinion might be, well it's no big deal."

I used to be angry. Now I'm just amused. I've been criticized for not being serious, that this page and my other writings and presentations about Zen are frivolous and trivial. Zen, I've been told, is a matter of life and death. Uh huh, sure. Tell that to my mom OK? What I'm saying here is more urgent than life and death. The world has got to change. People have got to wake up. This very instant. Right here. Right now, motherfuckers! Our survival depends on it. Truth doesn't give a fuck about us. If we don't get in line, the Truth will rub us right of the face of this planet.

But I don't think that's going to happen. A few people have got it. They grasp the Truth. When you grasp the Truth it's not like taking hold of some rock or jewel. You can't wrap your fist around it and then open up your palm and show it to everybody. It's like sticking your hand into a running stream and curling your fingers around the water. You can describe the coolness, the gentle caress it gives you. You can invite others to put their hands in too. If they do, they'll feel the same stream. You can't force it. And you can't try and accomplish anything by becoming anyone other than exactly who you are.

I'm not angry. I just talk nasty. You want world peace? You want to do something constructive? Sit down every day and stare at a blank wall. I'm not talking to bin Laden, George W. Bush, that idiot who shot a Pakistani gas station attendant. I'm talking to you. Find the source of war and the source of peace. They aren't far away. Peace won't be won by killing all the bad guys. Peace won't come from some new policy, a new political framework, a better way to redistribute the wealth. The cause of war isn't Those Bad Guys Way Over There. Don't worry about how you're going to convince those bad people to do good. Find the source for yourself. Get yourself together, then maybe you have a chance at changing Humanity. It's all right there inside you. You won't like what you see at first. But you have to dig down, all the way down to the source.

It's there. It's more you than you could ever be. Find it.

AFTERWORD

Ig Nition was the punk rock name of Robert Melvin Morningstar, the leader of the early eighties Kent, Ohio based punk rock band The F-Models.

The line about having been told that Zen was a matter of life and death refers to a fellow student of Nishijima Roshi who told me that my writings about Zen were not serious enough and that he considered Zen to be a matter of life and death. He was a long-time student of Nishijima's whose opinion I valued. It hurt to hear that especially because this Zen stuff was extremely serious to me.

Later on I decided that maybe saying "zen is punk" wasn't quite right.

Punk is Zen, Zen is Punk

CHAPTER 2

ZEN IS NOT PUNK

INTRODUCTION

This was written seven years after the "Zen is Punk" article as a sort of belated follow-up. A lot had happened in those seven years. For one thing, the idea that there was a connection between punk rock and Buddhism had started to become acceptable. When I first proposed it in the previous article I did not know of anyone—not a single person anywhere in the world—who saw any resemblance at all between punk and Buddhism. I was unaware of Noah Levine, whose book *Dharma Punx* had not yet been published. I had never met a single person in any Zen gathering I had attended in the near twenty years I'd been practicing who had the slightest interest in punk rock.

When I wrote the book that became *Hardcore Zen*, I believed there was no audience for it. I didn't even intend it for publication. Not when I was writing it, at least. After it was done I figured I had nothing to lose by sending it out to publishers the way I'd done with the novels I wrote before it. I assumed it would be rejected just like they were. I was stunned when Wisdom Publications said they wanted to put it out. I'm pretty sure they mainly did so because the buzz in the publishing industry at the time said that the forthcoming *Dharma Punx* would be a bestseller and Wisdom wanted their own punky Buddhist book to try and ride on some of the hype. I was double stunned when *Hardcore Zen* ended up selling very well. At least "very well" by the modest expectations for books about Zen.

Seven years later I felt it was important to point out that while zen was punk in some respects, it was also emphatically not punk as well. I felt like too many people were starting to imagine that they were precisely the same.

THE ARTICLE

Just over seven years ago I started writing about Buddhism on a website I called Sit Down and Shut Up. I'd been writing since high school and studying Zen since shortly after I got out of that hell. But until seven years ago I'd never felt confident writing about Zen. At that time I was rediscovering a lot of the punk rock musical and cultural stuff I'd been into nearly twenty years earlier. It seemed to me that my punk rock days had been much more important in my road to understanding Buddhism than I'd previously suspected.

So the first essay I wrote for that webpage was titled "Punk is Zen, Zen is Punk." The article isn't there anymore. But it was re-used as part of the opening of my first book, Hardcore Zen. The title was a reference to a line in the Heart Sutra that goes, "Form is emptiness, emptiness is form." That particular string of six words was my entry into Buddhist philosophy. When I first heard it I knew instantly it was right even though I didn't have a clue what it meant. Juxtaposing punk and Zen seemed to me a similar way of identifying two completely disparate concepts and finding the common ground between them, which, in this case, was me.

Somehow I seem to have built a career of sorts on identifying punk and Zen. But in the Zen philosophy also says, "Form is form and emptiness is emptiness." So it seems like time I finally come out and say that Zen is not punk and punk is not Zen, thereby possibly trashing my nascent writing career.

I'm up in Akron, Ohio now, where I've just finished playing three gigs with 0DFx (aka Zero Defex), the hardcore band I played bass for in '82-'83 and then again in 2005. We're also recording tracks for a CD we hope to put out in a few months. The experience of doing three punk rock shows and a bunch of punk rock recordings over the course of less than a week has brought home in no uncertain terms that in many very important ways punk rock is definitely not the same thing as Zen.

I felt this most strongly when we returned home from our show at Cleveland's Beachland Tavern with the amazing and mighty C.D. Truth (my new favorite band in the world) and the incredible Cheap Tragedies (best hardcore show I've ever seen in my life, go check 'em out if you get a chance). By the time we got done unloading all our gear it was four in the morning. When you're doing a Zen retreat you wake up at 4:30 AM and the contrast between the two lifestyles hit me like the big ol' cinder block our drummer Mickey X-Nelson uses to keep his kit from sliding around the stage. (We also did shows with Concordia Discors and Kill The Hippies, who both ruled.)

I tend to downplay the issue of discipline in my writing about Buddhist practice mainly because when I look at other Buddhist writing it seems like some people write about nothing but discipline. But it's a very important aspect of Buddhist practice to live in a regulated, disciplined way. You can't expect to maintain a balanced body and mind if you're continuously pulling yourself in eighteen directions at once by staying out late, sleeping in till a million o'clock, getting drunk and stoned, chasing tail and generally carousing. It just doesn't work.

This is a completely different attitude from the religious point of view that says stuff like that is sinful and evil. Sin and evil doesn't enter into it. It's just a simple fact that if you want your brain and body to work the way they're meant to, you need to take good care of the machinery that God gave you. No two ways about it.

At the same time, Buddhist practice isn't about being all austere and pure. Arbitrary designations of purity are useless. You know when your body and mind have been stretched and smashed and squeezed and pummeled just by paying attention to how you feel. And when I woke up way too fucking late this morning after a late night recording session with the mighty Defex at which beer and pot flowed freely—I didn't partake in either, but I'm extremely susceptible to contact highs and second-hand smoke—with my head throbbing and half the hearing gone out of my right ear I knew I'd been pushing things too far. Plus I realized when I was in the shower that this article was due today, not next week! Yikes. Pleaze excuse teh speeling mistekes.

While I was here in Ohio, though, I got to spend a time with my first Zen teacher, Tim McCarthy of the Kent Zendo. Watching him give his talk on Sunday morning reminded me what I really need to be doing. In answer to a question from a guy at the talk he said something like, "You couldn't exist without the whole of the Universe being just as it is and the whole of the Universe couldn't exist without you." The guy had been asking about whether Buddhists worship Buddha. Tim said, "So it's not really what you think of as worship. Instead you have a sense of awe and reverence for all things in the Universe. But at the same time you know that the Universe depends upon you. So it's a mutually reciprocal feeling." This is something all of us can tune into any time we wish. But most of us miss it entirely.

If I can help awaken that feeling in a few people, that's worth all the hardcore gigs in Ohio.

AFTERWORD

What a funny ending! I've always had a hard time with endings. I never liked the standard type endings they taught me to write in high school where you sum up what you just said. That feels repetitive. So sometimes I just end articles wherever they end.

This article seems to me now like two ideas fighting for space. And it probably was. As it says, the article was written in a big rush to meet a deadline. I do some of my best work that way. And even though the first half of this piece has little to do with the second half, it's still OK.

The main point of part one of this article is that Buddhist practice requires discipline. I felt like I'd been understating that a bit too much. The discipline required doesn't really need to be as militaristic as some people seem to believe. But you have to have some kind of discipline. Punk, on the other hand, is very loose. Yet, there again, you still need some measure of discipline to make punk work.

What makes punk punk to me is that punks take action. It's not enough to just dress funny. If you want to be truly punk, you have to do things. You have to put on shows, make records, make zines, create a scene, sustain that scene and so on. All of that takes discipline. Punks might look lazy to outsiders who don't understand them. But they're really not lazy at all.

So maybe I was wrong. Maybe punk is zen after all!

Of course, that's my whole point. It is and it isn't.

As for the second half, I found great inspiration in what Tim McCarthy said that Sunday morning and I still do. So I sort of shoehorned it into this article as a way of trying to make it available to a larger audience than the four people who were there to hear him say it. I hope maybe it does you some good too.

CHAPTER 3

BUDDHIST MUZAK

INTRODUCTION

I'm not certain why I decided to do a Buddhist webpage. I think it was mainly due to how disgusted I was with the other Buddhist webpages I'd seen during those days when the internet was still relatively new. They were all so nice and inoffensive.

It wasn't that they just avoided using bad words. It was more that they did not challenge the reader in any way. They didn't probe deeply into anything. Rather, they were like lullabies, intended to soothe the reader into a dull, dreamy state. This was quite unlike the Buddhism I'd been living with for, by then, about twenty years.

That Buddhism was hard edged. It asked questions. It provided no easy place of rest. It challenged. It was acerbic, astringent, sometimes downright nasty. This was exemplified by books like *Zen Mind Beginner's Mind* by Shunryu Suzuki or *To Meet The Real Dragon* by my teacher Gudo Nishijima. These books used no dirty words. They would have received a PG or even a G rating. Yet they were not soothing, quieting, or stilling in any way.

They pointed to a state of unshakable stability and deep quiet. But this state was not far away. It was right here, underlying everything we do, everything we are. We didn't need to run away from our real lives in order to find this state. We didn't need to alter our consciousness with chemicals or weird mental gymnastics. We just needed to pay attention to who we were and where we were.

The webpages I was reading, though, seemed to imply that we had to go elsewhere and seek something higher, something better, something "more pure" than the supposedly mundane world we were living in right now. They wanted their readers to turn away from what was real and escape with them into a world of pretty fantasy.

At the time I didn't feel like I was up to the task of presenting a different perspective. But I also felt that a different perspective needed to be presented and nobody else was doing it. So I decided to make an attempt.

This is it.

THE ARTICLE

It's really sad that people have come to believe Buddhist writing should function like elevator music.

A kind of standard has emerged in the past 30 years or so that defines for most people what Buddhist writing ought to be like. Buddhist writing, it's widely assumed, should have a calming, soothing, stilling effect upon its readers. This standard has been so widely accepted that people think Buddhism is only Buddhism when it's presented in this way. But that's just Buddhism by Hallmark. It has nothing at all to do with real Buddhism.

Mix up some lullaby style writing with a few well-worn Buddhist clichés and you get a potent mixture—habit forming and definitely mind altering. Its effect is the same brainless zoned out state you can get from over-exposure to video games, hours of net surfing or vegging out in front of the tube. It's the stillness of a corpse, the quiet that comes when you plug up your ears to the sounds of the real world. The inner peace of Buddhism has nothing at all to do with the numbing, paralyzing, near comatose effect the average so-called "Buddhist" writing has on its readers.

Real peace and quietude is vibrantly alive. It is the peace that is the wellspring of life itself.

There is little that is quieting in Dogen's writing. Nor is there is Nagarjuna's writings or in the recorded lectures of Gautama Buddha himself. Far from being quieting, they're energetic, challenging, arousing, even provocative. If you find these writers calming you aren't reading them very carefully. They're positively unsettling. Freddy Kreuger is nothing compared to Dogen.

Writing is a type of thought. All writing. Real stillness can never be found in thought. Writing that invokes the feeling of stillness and quiet is just invoking dead memories of pleasant times when you may have touched real stillness. The belief that a piece of writing can produce real stillness in its readers is as reasonable as believing a dead body could get up and dance and sing. Writing simply cannot do that any more than a finger pointing at the moon can be the moon itself. If you think that what you're getting when you read that trash is the Buddhist state or Zen Consciousness, remember Johnny Rotten's immortal words at the end of the Sex Pistols' last gig*. "Ever have the feeling you've been cheated?"

I know about this because I used to be a great fan of such writing. I had a massive collection of soothing, quieting "Buddhist" books. Lovely things they were too. True works of art. Any kind of work or art will have some effect on the body and mind of the person who enjoys it. The film *Voyage to the Planet of Prehistoric Women* is the most quieting and lovely work of art I know. I'm being very serious here. Those stodgy Soviet Cosmonauts encountering fat brontosauruses as they trudge through the swamps of planet Venus, that haunting ethereal Theremin music, Mamie Van Doren and a dozen stoned hippy chicks in sea shell bikinis, what could possibly be more soothing?
Trash science fiction isn't Buddhism. That's easy to see. I feel very lucky to have such oddball tastes. When I tell people the things

I find soothing and beautiful, I get no support at all. But if your tastes are more mainstream, you'll find millions of people ready to support you when you tell them what you find peaceful and relaxing. And since peaceful and relaxing is what most people figure Buddhism is all about, there's a world full of people who'll agree when you say that those things are what Buddhism is all about. That social reinforcement can be very powerful.

There are, in fact, some Universals in this area. Buddhist temples in China and Japan are designed in an almost scientific way to invoke feelings of peace in those who enter them. The building materials, colors, the use of space and so on are all chosen for maximum calming effect the same way the same elements are chosen for precisely the opposite effect when building a Vegas casino. The sights, sounds and scents of nature evoke feelings of calm and well being. That's why most Buddhist temples are high up on green hillsides, next to babbling brooks and far from the noise and pollution of the city. Double whammy.

All that peace and calm is a bit of a cheat, though. It's a come-on, like a hooker flashing you a bit of leg. She's not lying. Not exactly. That leg really is a lovely thing. And when it's wrapped around your back it will feel very nice indeed. But it's going to cost you. You might get caught by the cops or by your spouse, or catch some terrible disease. You're risking a hell of a lot for that little bit of leg. Buddhist temples are like that. They show you a little taste of inner peace. But most of them won't tell you how high a price you're going to have to pay to make that peace your own. They sure won't tell you it's going to kill you.

Some reasonable Buddhist writers use this rather deceptive technique. But the really good ones avoid it. And there are a busload of dopes who think they've got the whole Buddhist shebang nailed down tight when all they really know is what it feels like to zone out while sitting in the lotus position.

They're ready to tell you all about it, too. Step right up!

Folks travel down this path for years and years and most of them never come back. Again, I should know. And I'm grateful to the teachers I've had who whacked me over the head (metaphorically) whenever I got that glassy-eyed look of phony inner peace that comes from reading such things.

I vividly recall one time telling my first Buddhist teacher, Tim about how beautiful and quieting I found the works of a certain writer of books on Eastern mysticism. "Oh yeah," he replied, his voice dripping with sarcasm, "Mister Love!" Nishijima Roshi's lectures used to make me so mad there'd be steam coming out of my ears. Here I was coming from a background of punk rock—all thrashing guitars, slam dancing and shouted obscenities at the establishment. Yet I found these so-called "spiritual masters" incredibly abrasive.

Whenever I thought I'd found "it," they were right there to tell me I was just being stupid. Once I had a very profound vision, a vision that I thought to be the culmination, the crowning glory of my years of studying and practice. Nishijima Roshi put me down in a way that almost had me in tears. At that moment his words weren't the least bit calming. But it was the most truly Buddhist thing he could possibly have done.

There's a lovely scene in the book *Shoes Outside The Door* by Michael Downing. Downing's intent is, I think, to show what a callous and nasty little man Richard Baker, former abbot of the San Francisco Zen Center, was. One of Baker's long time students comes to him with this wonderful description of a very profound enlightenment experience. After he's done, Baker asks, "Can you shoot energy up through your spine?" The poor guy is heart-broken. He's done all this wonderfully advanced spiritual stuff and all his beloved Zen Master can do is knock him down with a challenge to do something he can't. What this scene really shows, though, is that, in spite of his other faults, Baker could be a very good Zen teacher indeed when he wanted to be.

If I seem loud it's because I'm trying to shout over the noise and confusion of repeated exposure to things that are "quiet" in that phony way. If you think you know what stillness is, you don't at all. Stillness knows what you are. It never goes the other way around. Not for a second. Not for an instant.

Human beings are all fundamentally the same. The few differences we do have —both outside and inside—are incredibly superficial. There is more genetic variation in two chimpanzees from the same forest than there is in two human beings from opposite sides of the Earth. It seems we're hardly even a species in the way that most animals are. We're more of a huge extended family. And so the writings of Dogen and Nagarjuna and the recorded lectures of Gautama Buddha, are all full of massive sweeping generalizations. All good Buddhist writings are. Folks don't like to hear generalizations because they'd rather dwell on their own petty and meaningless little differences than to get right down to what really matters.

If you want stilling, quieting stuff that reinforces all of your silly little habits and personality quirks, there's plenty to go around. I feel a kind of duty to tear this stuff apart. It's a pretty stupid road to choose. I'd get a lot fewer complaints if I just wrote in the standard fashion. But that's a waste of time. What I've chosen to do instead is get right up people's noses. "It's the hard way. The long way," Nishijima Roshi told me about this approach, "but it needs to be done."

*not counting the "just for the money" reunion of the mid 90's of course.

32

AFTERWORD

These days I wouldn't assume my readers were familiar with films like *Voyage to the Planet of Prehistoric Women* or even books like *Shoes Outside the Door* the way I seem to be doing in this piece. I'd explain what they were or at least put in links to webpages about them. But you can look that stuff up if you're interested.

Reading this again I can see why people found my early writing struck people as arrogant and conceited. I guess people still find me insufferable. But I don't think "conceited" or "arrogant" are the right words for what this guy is trying to express.

I have a certain degree of insight into the Brad Warner of ten years ago that other readers don't. He's clumsy and lacks any sense of subtlety. But he knows this, so he doesn't even attempt to be subtle. He isn't saying he's better than you. Even though he sounds like it. I know very well the incredible inferiority complex he suffered from then, and still suffers from now. His advise is meant as much for himself as for anyone else. In fact he probably didn't think anyone else was reading this stuff anyway!

That being said, I still cringe when I read my own early writing sometimes. This particular piece is really grating. I can see that now. I could probably see that then too. I just didn't care.

I'm glad I wrote stuff like this. When Wisdom Publications edited *Hardcore Zen* they took out a lot of the more acerbic material and made the whole thing much more palatable. This did wonders for book sales. But I felt like it made the book weaker. The again, maybe that was OK.

CHAPTER 4

LOSING MY RELIGION

INTRODUCTION

Because I started my Zen webpage sometime in the late summer of 2001 and decided to update it once a week one of the very first pieces of news I ever wrote about in a Zen context was the terrorist attack on New York on September 11, 2001.

I can't find that article anymore. But I remember that I blamed the events of that day squarely on religion. Not on some particular religion, mind you, but on religion itself. I said that it was the religious impulse that had caused that tragedy. It was my contention that the belief that spirit was more real than matter was at the heart of what drove those maniacs to do what they did that day. I get more into what I mean by this in the article below.

After I posted that original piece about religion being the root cause of the September 11th tragedy, a good friend of mine reacted very strongly to it. Religion, she said, had saved her life. How could I call into question people's belief in a Higher Power?

It wasn't my intention to say that there was no God. In fact I believe in God. I just think religions have it all wrong about God. They think God is pure spirit. That makes no sense. Even if you follow the traditional Christian ideas about God, you're still left with God having to create the universe out of something. Since God was the only thing that existed before the creation (at least according to this idea) how could God create the universe out of anything other than his own substance? I don't believe that scenario of the creation anyway. I just offer that argument as yet another line of reasoning against the idea of God being pure spirit.

In any case, the article below was written in part as a way to try to explain to the person who wrote to me why I had said what I said about September 11th. I don't think she ever read it. But maybe she did.

THE ARTICLE

Of all the stuff I say on this page, the one thing that people seem to get most upset about—even more than masturbation, even more than dirty words, even more than references to the Zen aspects of the film *Voyage to the Planet of Prehistoric Women* (a classic!)—is when I say bad stuff about religion. So I thought I'd write something about what religion is and why Buddhism isn't one.

There are plenty of Buddhists who will tell you Buddhism is a religion. And I would agree with some of them. It all depends what you mean by the word "religion." In its purest sense the word religion just refers to anything that helps people establish a relationship with God. In this sense, Buddhism could be called a religion. But that's not what the word religion means to most of us.

To me, a religion is a social organization based on the illusion of a common belief system amongst its members. As I've said before, no two human beings can hold exactly the same beliefs. In fact it's rare to find any one human being who can hold the exact same set of beliefs from one moment to the next. Those who try to do so end up driving themselves mad. It's unnatural to hold consistent beliefs. All belief, to paraphrase the guru in the Monkees movie *Head**, is the result of conditioning (why is that Hollywood guru so much wiser than any of the real ones?). We believe what we believe because we've been conditioned to do so, rewarded since birth by society for espousing what society considers the correct beliefs, or rewarded by our peers when we reject the wider society's beliefs for theirs. Deep down, though, society has no idea what its own beliefs really are or where they come from.

Religions are concerned with man's spiritual side. Let's go into that a little bit. All of the world's philosophies and religions, with one exception, make a very clear distinction between spirit and matter. This distinction is so deeply embedded in all the world's cultures that we take it for granted as a real thing. Religions disregard the material side of life and concentrate only on the spiritual. Everything they do in the material realm is for the benefit of the spirit. God is a spirit who created the material world. We are spirits in the material world, to quote Sting. Our real being is the spirit which inhabits our flesh and when that flesh dies the spirit will depart, either to Heaven or Hell or to go off and get stuck into another fleshly body. Matter is temporary. Spirit is eternal. So it only makes sense to favor spirit.

There are those who believe that our society has become too materialistic, that the way to get things right is to return to earlier more spiritual views. This is a mistake. The early spiritual views failed. That's why we abandoned them. But now we're starting to wake up to the fact that materialism is a failure too. We know that people who achieve every benefit the material world has to offer are just as miserable as anyone else (we should thank our celebrity gossip magazines for helping us understand this, I'm serious here folks). We don't need a return to spiritualism any more than we need to become more materialistic.

As belief in the reality of spirit faded in the west, the philosophy of materialism took hold. Science has shown us beyond any doubt that matter is real. Religions are no longer convincing. So we've come to believe that spirit is just an illusion. Our material brains work in a certain way, which gives us the illusion of spirit. People try to fight this belief in a lot of ways because it's a frightening, lonely thing to believe. But science works so very well, it's nearly impossible to avoid.

Here's where Buddhism comes in to rescue us. The reason we hate to believe that science is right is because we believe so deeply in the division of matter and spirit. If the material view is right—and who can deny that it is anymore?—we think we can't believe in anything spiritual. The two sides are fundamentally opposed. If one is right, the other is wrong.

As much as we understand that matter is real (but not reality, I'll get to that in a minute), we can't deny spirit. When we cry, who feels sad? When we get angry at some idiot writing a web page, who feels anger? Our spiritual side is very real. But so is matter. This is because they're the exact same thing. A scientific type might like that idea because it fits with his view that spirit is just an illusion created by the coming together of material elements. A Buddhist would agree with that. But, when a scientist stubs his toe on a Bunsen burner someone left on the floor, who shouts in pain? This is a very mysterious thing and all the science in the world can't explain it to anyone's satisfaction.

Neither can religions.

The problem is that both sides come at the issue the wrong way. We aren't just spirits. We have physical bodies with physical needs. We can't pretend they don't count And we aren't just robots made out of meat who only think we're alive. Life is real.

We don't need to choose one or the other. Reality isn't matter and reality isn't spirit. Reality isn't what we perceive and it isn't what we think. Reality includes both and by including both goes beyond either of these elements alone. Reality exists before our attempts to explain it as matter or as spirit. The truth exists before we give it a name. The truth exists even if we call it the wrong name, even if we explain it as something it's not.

Buddhism is not about belief and it's not about emphasizing spirit over matter. Buddhism is what exists before belief appears. Buddhism is prior to matter and prior to spirit.

Buddhism doesn't ask you to believe in anything at all except reality itself. These days "reality" and "realism" are often used as synonyms for matter and materialistic beliefs. In this view, reality is only what we perceive with our senses. But that's not the Buddhist view of reality. Reality exists prior to our physical senses. Reality includes things we cannot sense physically. Reality remains when our senses are impaired. Yet reality has a physical side and we can never deny that, as religions say we can. Buddha discovered this when he tried to become spiritually enlightened by denying his physical needs. He got thin and weak and delirious. By denying his physical reality the best he could hope for was a painful death. That's a far cry from enlightenment.

Buddhism is a philosophy of action. It is the only philosophy of action. What we actually do is the fundamental point, not what we think and not what we perceive. Zazen is the fundamental Buddhist action. Buddhism cannot be understood without the practice of Zazen. Those who try to do so will fail every time.

Zazen is not meditation. It is not a spiritual practice. It has nothing to do with belief. I once heard from a born-again Christian that Zazen is dangerous because if you empty your mind of thoughts demons will take over your body. Hey, there have been times while doing Zazen that I've wished demons would appear and try to take over my body! Anything to lessen the boredom! Zazen is beyond all beliefs. Zazen will be what it will be in spite of whatever beliefs you hold about it. Or about anything else.

But beware. Zazen will bring you right down to the very source of your beliefs. And when you get there, you might not be able to believe them anymore.

* For those of you who want to know, the speech given by the guru from the Monkees movie Head (played by Abraham Sofaer) goes like this: "We were speaking of belief and conditioning. All belief could be said to be the result of some sort of conditioning. A psychologically tested belief of our time is that the central nervous system, which feeds its impulses directly to the brain, the conscious and the subconscious, is unable to differentiate between the real and the vividly imagined experience. If there is a difference. And most of us believe there is. Am I being clear? For to examine these concepts requires tremendous energy and discipline. To allow the unknown to occur and to occur requires clarity. For where there is clarity there is no choice. And where there is choice there is misery. But why should anyone listen to me, since I know nothing?" I memorized this speech when I decided to dress up as that guru for Halloween in 1985.

AFTERWORD

Not much to say after this one. I've put this idea in one form or another into every book I've written. It was the cornerstone of the philosophy I learned from Gudo Nishijima Roshi. I'm indebted to him for this particular reading of Buddhist philosophy. But the idea is not his. It's there in the core of the earliest teachings of Buddhism. Nishijima's only innovation was to link it to the contemporary Western terms materialism and idealism. And he probably wasn't even the first to do this.

I was never that much of a student of Western philosophy. So it took me a while of listening to Nishijima to get a handle on what he meant when he said idealism. Materialism I got pretty much off the bat. But idealism was tougher.

I understood the term only in its more common usage in which to be idealistic meant something like to be optimistic or even enthusiastic about changing bad situations into good ones. The dictionary on the word processing program I'm using to type this says that one definition of an idealist is "somebody who aspires to or lives in accordance with high standards or principles." I didn't understand why anyone would be against that.

But that isn't the sense in which Nishijima Roshi usually used the word. He used the word idealist in a way more like another sense that my dictionary gives, "somebody who rejects practical considerations in pursuit of perfection." But even more than that he used it more according to the third and last definition my dictionary gives, "a believer in a philosophy that material objects do not exist independently of the mind."

Now the way that's phrased makes it sound something like Buddhism. Buddhists don't believe matter exists independently of mind. But idealists tend to go further and think that the mind or spirit is more real than matter. This is the basis of most religions. God, who is pure spirit, is more real than us. Our spiritual souls are more real than our material bodies. Lots of religions say this explicitly. Lots of others imply this without ever really stating it.

It's that sort of idealism Nishijima was arguing against.

As for the other sort of idealism, Nishijima was always talking about how he was an optimist and said he was constantly striving to improve himself. He certainly aspired to and live according to high standards and principles. So in that sense maybe one could call him idealistic. Although I'm sure he wouldn't like it!

CHAPTER 5

THE SOURCE OF ALL RELIGION

INTRODUCTION

I know what I was trying to say with this piece. I'm not sure if I said it or not.

Re-reading it now I realize my understanding of who Mother Theresa was and what she did was a little shallow. Not that I have a very deep understanding of her now. But at the time I just thought of her as a completely saintly person dedicated to eradicating suffering at the expense of her personal comfort and with no thought of a reward for herself.

I don't know how true that was anymore. Maybe it was. But her views on birth control certainly did some damage. And Christopher Hitchens argued that Mother Theresa wasn't working to alleviate poverty and suffering but to expand the number of Catholic converts in the world. Maybe so. But overall I'd still say her charitable work was pretty exemplary. And I think it's clear that it's the mythical sense of Mother Theresa that I'm talking about here rather than who she might have "really" been if anyone can be reduced to such terms.

THE ARTICLE

Let's say you went to Paris and saw the Eiffel Tower. Now you meet me and try to describe what you've seen. If I've never seen the Eiffel Tower, your description is going to be very difficult for me to follow. It's not shaped like most other buildings I've seen, so the image your words create in my mind is going to be a little off at best. In the case of so-called religious matters this kind of thing gets especially challenging. Everyone has very strong ideas about religion. So you're trying to describe the Eiffel Tower to me when I already have a very detailed image in my mind of what the Eiffel Tower looks like. In fact, my image is so very precise I cannot differentiate it from the Eiffel Tower itself. There's nothing you can say to me to prove that what I think is the Eiffel Tower is nothing more than a mental construction.

One day you may come upon the source of all religion. Not the source of Buddhism, Christianity, Hinduism, Voodoo, Wicca, the Church of the Sub Genius or whatever, but the true source of mankind's religious impulse. It won't be words in a book (or on a web page). It won't be an old guy on a throne, or a blue dude with four arms, or a great big ball of light. But you will know it for what it is instantly. You won't be able to doubt it any more than you can doubt the existence of your own nose. Yet you won't be able to describe it at all, even to yourself. But if you're very skillful, you might be able to draw a map so someone else can get there. Or, if you're like me, you'll draw maps like the ones at Japanese train stations. No one I know, Japanese or foreign, can ever figure those out.

The biggest problem in describing this stuff is that we tend to think that the source of all religion is a mental construction. Believers think this mental construction can be expressed precisely in words and they know exactly which words are right. The words are the religion. Unbelievers think that all mental constructions are pretty much equal so none of the existing ones have any particular advantage over the competition. Since the words can't be trusted, religion must be false. Both sides are wrong because the source of religion is not a mental construction at all.

Why do people imagine that the source of religion can be adequately described verbally? Forget it. Nothing can really be adequately described with words. If I tell you "I saw a tree," this doesn't really transmit the full experience to you. Even if I could transmit my memory of seeing that tree directly into your mind, memory itself is just another kind of symbolic language. It's a personal language that only one person can "speak," but it's a symbolic language nonetheless. The memory is not the experience. We don't store our experiences. They're gone forever. You should laugh at anyone who uses the phrase "I have experience." The past, our own cherished past, is unreal, a phantom. Go rent Total Recall (a poor adaptation of Philip K. Dick's brilliant short story "We Can Remember It For You Wholesale").

Once you have visited the source of all religion you could keep its location to yourself. But you'll see so many people suffering in such unnecessary ways simply because they don't know the source of religion (and of their own suffering) that your natural human compassion comes to the fore. If what you've seen is the true source of all religion, you won't be trying to convince anyone of anything. You won't proselytize or evangelize. If you feel the need to convince anyone you're right, you've already gone wrong. And you will never offer the source to anyone who has not asked for it.

Then there's the Mother Theresa thing. That one's a tough nut to crack. I thought of her as I was writing that bit last week about how religious people do what they do just to benefit their souls and not out of concern for the world's material situation. What Mother Theresa did was so wonderful and so very selfless and compassionate that her behavior has become a symbol for right action above any other. This is a mistake.

When I was younger, I looked at what I really wanted to do in life, things like make music or work in the film industry. Then I saw

Mother Theresa and others like her. How could I do something so frivolous as playing guitar or making films when I should be out in India helping the starving children? So I ended up working at a workshop for the mentally handicapped. It was a very pure, selfless sort of job where I got to change the diapers on 6 foot tall men who thought the whole thing was a very fun game or get hit on the head by a marble table lamp thrown by a 35 year old pre-verbal man having a bad day. The pay was lousy too. Good lord, I hated it.

Was that the Right Livelihood Buddha spoke about? It was for some of the people who worked there. They loved it. Would being a professional musician really have been wrong? There were times in my teens when pieces of music were the only things that kept me from throwing myself off a bridge. Would the world really have been better off if John Lennon or Pete Townshend had decided to dedicate their energies to something more "selfless" like delivering medicine to disease stricken Malaysians or digging irrigation ditches in West Africa?

Doing something you really care about is far more important than conforming to some idea if right livelihood. I'm sure Mother Theresa understood this. But her example is often trotted out by people who do not. There is suffering everywhere. Starving Afghan refugees ought to get relief. But there are people right next to you who need the kind of relief only you can give them as much as those poor Afghans need fresh water and shoes. Don't deprive them of what you have to give.

What I found in my previous job is that a lot of people who seem very selfless and saintly are more a part of the problem than a part of the solution. They help the underprivileged in order to make themselves feel superior and end up creating more misery in order to have someone to "help." There are certainly exceptions to this. And I met some wonderful ones. But they were the minority, I'm afraid. This is a very subtle thing and even speaking about it can get people really cranky at you.

I've seen this first hand. But here's the part that'll really make you mad: I do not have to see these things first hand to understand them completely. Doesn't that sound arrogant? But look into yourself deeply and you will find that you, yes even you, have this kind of desire. Just like I do. You're a big old butt-in-ski whose main motivation for altruistic behavior is to inflate your own ego. Again, just like me. How many Boy Scouts does it take to walk an old lady across the street? Six. Why so many? Because she didn't want to go.

You are the world. You do not need to read the Bible and every Dead Sea Scroll to find the true source of Christianity. Jesus didn't and neither did his disciples. They wrote those books to describe what they'd actually experienced. But the books were not the experience any more than the words "I stepped in a big pile of dog do" is the experience of stepping in dog do.

Whatever desires exist in you exist in everyone everywhere and vice-versa. The degree to which these desires manifest themselves varies from person to person. That's all a "personality" really is. That may be all a "person" really is (and I include the physical being as well here). You can understand Mother Theresa or Osama bin Laden perfectly. This is a difficult point. The sickest most twisted psychotic sociopath lives inside you. Right next to him are Gandhi, Martin Luther King and Siddhartha. People think you need to study a person's life in great detail before you can understand him or her. You need to study to get knowledge of something like that. But real understanding is instantaneous because the one you understand is yourself.

If you say you have arrived at the source of all religions, it sounds like very big talk. Naturally people will want to see some proof.

You won't have any. Not a shred. They don't sell souvenirs there the way they do on the road up to Eiheiji monastery. There are people who have tried to devise systems to prove stuff like this. But those systems always degenerate into foolishness. The source of religion is not bound by authority or social standing. It's not to be found in the past or the future. The source of religion is in each and every one of us. You can't show it to me. I have to find it for myself.

You can't stay too long at the source of religion. You can't live there. It would make you dizzy. But if you visit that place once, you can never forget it. Not in this lifetime or in a thousand lifetimes. Dogen said "it manifests traces of forgotten realization for a long, long time." Once you know the way, you can return whenever you like. At the same time, that place is the source of you as well. So you never really leave it.

The place where I first noticed the source of all religion is a spot I pass at least twice every weekday on my way to work and on my way home again. It wasn't somewhere far away, although when I was a teenager in Wadsworth, Ohio, a street running along the banks of the Sengawa River in Tokyo certainly would have seemed impossibly distant. The place where you first find it won't be exotic either. Visiting the Holy Lands or meditating under the tree where Buddha had his life changed by the sight of Venus rising in the morning sky would be as futile as visiting my dirty street corner in Tokyo. You won't find it where I found it and when you see it, you'll see your face in the sky, not mine. But you'll notice not even a single pore is the least bit different. It will be more you than you ever could be.

If I sound arrogant, like I'm claiming some special knowledge or some great experience, please forgive me. What I've seen (what I see) is ordinary beyond the ordinary. I have looked at my own mundane life as it really is and noticed it is nothing other than the Promised Land.

The source of all religion is right here. You couldn't get away from it if you tried to. There is nowhere else to go.

(*Special thanx to Dan'l Danehy-Oakes for his comments on this page & for the joke about the Boy Scouts*)

AFTERWORD

A big sigh here.

This article references something I'd put up earlier on my web page and which I later rewrote and put in my book *Hardcore Zen*. And that something was a piece I wrote about an experience I had while walking along the Sengawa River in Tokyo on my way to work. It was an experience others have called *kensho* or enlightenment after reading what I wrote about it. I try to avoid words like that because I don't know what people mean when they use them.

I suppose the piece above sounds like I'm subtly claiming I have some kind of special knowledge or experience even as it overtly claims I do not. Yet there's no other way to talk about this stuff. The common solution to this dilemma in Soto style Zen has been not to talk about it at all. But I've already started talking about it and now I'm stuck with my own past karma. I feel like it needs to be discussed, even though such discussions inevitably go wrong.

My experience, to use the dreaded word "experience" that I denounced in the article, is obviously uncommon. I can't deny that. Although it is available to absolutely everyone, few of us are willing to do the work involved in changing our habitual thoughts and actions enough to make our true nature visible to ourselves.

In some sense I am guilty of the terrible sin of talking about this experience in order to lend some kind of credence to the other things I say. I know people place value on those who've had experiences like this because I did and sometimes still do.

But you've got to be careful. There is plenty of literature out there about experiences like this and there has been for thousands of years. So it's easy for someone to make it up. It's also easy for people to have very shallow insights and blow them up into something extraordinary. Perhaps I'm doing so myself. Plenty of people have said that I am. And I have no way to argue against them without making myself sound even more ridiculous than I already have.

This is why the experiences of others don't really matter all that much. It's what you experience for yourself that counts.

The Source of All Religion

CHAPTER 6

HOPELESSLY NAIVE

INTRODUCTION

This is a rant. I can understand completely why people assume I'm angry when they read this kind of stuff. But I swear to God I never write when I'm angry. It takes a lot of work to get a rant like this together. It's impossible to do that kind of work when you're pissed off.

On the other hand I suppose there is and will always be an undercurrent of anger in me. It's the way I relate to the world. But that's a different kind of thing. That's an aspect of my personality.

This is a totally different thing from being pissed off right now. When Buddhism talks about refraining from anger it's talking about refraining from lashing out in emotional displays. It's not talking about erasing anger from your personality. Dogen certainly didn't do that.

THE ARTICLE

The world is in deep shit and the only solution I have to all of our current woes is hopelessly naive. In times of crisis like these, people want big solutions. They want to hear about security measures, troop deployment, sweeping policy changes. Wanna hear my solution? It's morality.

The morality I'm talking about has nothing to do with religions or beliefs. It's not based on the fear of punishment by God, or even of Karmic retribution. There are no lists of do's and don't's. The kind of morality we need has to come from each individual, but it is not based on our own personal ideas of what is right and what is wrong. It isn't an "I make my own rules, man!" morality. Morality has nothing whatsoever to do with rules, either yours or someone else's. The kind of morality I'm talking about is based on a single criteria; right action in the present moment.

Morality isn't just about big things like killing or stealing. Morality includes everything you do in your life. It includes the way you interact with your coworkers, the way you pay your utility bills, the way you deal with the driver who cuts you off on the freeway. It includes the way you eat and sleep and how you dress yourself (a spiky green mohawk and a studded jacket may be as moral as a suit and tie).

God may indeed punish us when we do wrong. But to call it "punishment," to call the source of punishment "God" and to view God as a kind of person like ourselves only causes confusion. God is the Universe in both its physical and its non-physical manifestations. Universal Law can never be violated. Another way of saying this is that the law of cause and effect is absolute. It makes no sense to fear punishment from God. God is the source of you and you are the source of God. You can understand natural laws and refrain from doing stupid things, the same way you understand the law of gravity and refrain from dropping bowling balls on your feet. The realm of human interaction has natural laws just like the rest of the Universe.

We tend to believe people can do wrong and get away with it, even profit from it. But I see no reason to accept such a belief. How can I say that, you ask. Right now there are mass murderers living in palaces with all the money in the world at their disposal while good men and women suffer from poverty, disease and hunger.

I say this because I have observed how cause and effect operate in my own life. I have seen that when I take even the slightest deviation from the rule of the universe (and I do this quite often), I suffer for it to exactly the degree to which I deviated. You know the law of the Universe through your own joy and your own suffering. Your soul is the soul of every sentient being in the Universe and what applies to you applies to everyone. A mass murderer may end up as a rich man, but he suffers the pains of Hell in his mansion. If he tries to ignore the pain it only becomes greater until it cannot be ignored any longer.
Open your eyes.

The interesting thing is that the more clearly you understand the law of cause and effect, the faster the law operates. This is God's mercy. In actual fact, cause and effect operate simultaneously. The cause is the effect. But if we are deluded, things may seem to take a very long time to have any effect. That's why our rich murderer thinks he's gotten away with something. He hasn't, he's just too stupid to see how he's being affected by what he did. The degree of our delusion may determine how long it takes to notice the effects we generate.

If you want to really change the world, you have to start with yourself. You have to look at your own action right here and right now. You are the only one you can ever change. And don't think it's going to be easy. Your opinions, your beliefs, your traditions, the habits you picked up from your family and your culture, are all of no value at all when it comes to true morality.

All you have to do is learn to observe yourself clearly and with penetrating honesty—the kind of honesty that melts right through your own most thoroughly built up defenses (it hurts, believe me, but it's good for you). Any person can learn it, but some people never will. They're too cowardly to even entertain such an idea. Don't worry about those people. Your duty is to help create a climate where those people can no longer operate. We're closer than we have ever been before.

AFTERWORD

I wouldn't say any of this now the way I did when I wrote this. But I still feel essentially the same way.

These rants are rants at myself and my own tendency to be stupid. They're not really meant to be anything other than that. But in phrasing things the way I did at the time I wrote this, I made it seem like I was coming from a higher position and denouncing those below me. I regret that. It wasn't my intention to give that impression.

The guy who wrote this piece—Brad of however many years ago—sounds harsh and unforgiving. I was trying to indicate my feeling that the Universe itself is absolutely unforgiving. The law of cause and effect won't respond to our excuses. There's nothing to appeal to.

But the law of cause and effect is also perfectly just in its own way. Effect only follows cause. A big cause produces a big effect, a small cause produces a small effect.

The reason this piece is called "Hopelessly Naïve" is because it comes close to expressing what a lot of people call the "just world hypothesis." According to Wikipedia, "The just-world hypothesis (also called the just-world theory, just-world fallacy, just-world effect, or just-world phenomenon) refers to the tendency for people to want to believe that the world is fundamentally just. As a result, when they witness an otherwise inexplicable injustice, they will rationalize it by searching for things that the victim might have done to deserve it. This deflects their anxiety, and lets them continue to believe the world is a just place, but often at the expense of blaming victims for things that were not, objectively, their fault."

I don't really believe in the just world hypothesis as such. I certainly don't believe in blaming victims for things that were not their fault. The difference between what I'm saying here and the so-called "just world hypothesis" is that the just world hypothesis applies outwardly. I only apply my beliefs about the justice of the universe to myself. I don't look at a child with a horrible genetic disorder and imagine that she must have done something awful in a past life. That sort of speculation is useless. When confronted with someone like that, you do what you can do to help. You don't worry about the rest.

Yet in my own life I accept that I reap exactly what I sow. Still, I don't bother too much speculating about things that are unknown and unknowable. I'm not interested in doing past life regressions to see why I was born to a mother who died of Huntington's Disease. It's irrelevant. It wouldn't help me to know. Why should I waste time trying to find out?

CHAPTER 7

NOTHING IS SACRED (NOTHING IS PROFANE)

INTRODUCTION

Those of you who have read my book *Hardcore Zen* will recognize this. I used most of it in the book. I have a number of pieces like this, ones that I rewrote and put into books. But I figured an e-book of just those would be boring and redundant.

Still, I'm the kind of guy who buys reissues of CDs I already have in order to get bonus tracks that usually consist of demo versions of songs I already own. So this is for anyone out there who is the same way about books. Think of this as the demo version of that passage from *Hardcore Zen*. It will give you an idea what that book was like before the folks at Wisdom Publications turned it into something more palatable to general readership.

THE ARTICLE

Nothing is sacred. Doubt is absolutely essential. Everything, no matter how great, how fundamental, how beautiful or important it is, must be questioned. It is only when people believe that something is above questioning, beyond all doubt, that they can be as truly horrible as we all know they can be.

Everything is sacred. Every blade of grass, every cockroach, every speck of dust, every flower, every turd floating in pool of mud outside a graffiti splattered housing project is God. Everything is a worthy object of worship.

Everything is profane. Saving the planet is a waste of time and energy. Motherly love is useless. Flowers are ugly. My uncle Scott fell into a deep depression and drank himself to death. I visited him a few months before he died and heard him complain that the birds chirping outside his window were noisy and irritating. Scott was a lovely guy. When I was a kid, I used to look forward to seeing him whenever we visited his place. He made me laugh. He treated us kids as real people. I always try to treat children the way Scott treated me. Singing birds are irritating noise.

Nothing is profane. Not even you.

If we hold anything sacred we are treading down a very danger-ous path. And by "anything" I mean anything. Last year the world saw what was at the end of that path. But most people haven't re-ally grasped the lesson. The lesson wasn't that what those people held sacred was wrong, and that there are other things worth holding scared. The lesson is that you must hold nothing sacred unless you can hold everything sacred. God is everything. You cannot possibly worship Him if you can't worship every last one of His creations, His manifestations.

Buddha's truth screams at you from billboard cigarette ads. God's voice sings to you in elevator Muzak®. It announces itself when you step on a discarded candy bar wrapper. It rains on you from the sky above. You eat the Buddhist Truth and poop it out four hours later. What a lovely fragrance the Dharma has! If you ran away as fast as you could for the rest of your life you couldn't pos-sibly escape Reality.

Nothing is Sacred (Nothing is Profane)

So why are you wasting your time looking for it here?

Why do I bother trying to write for people who never even read?
You're not going to get this. Go away. Don't bug me. I'm typing
just to keep my fingers from getting cold. It's not for you at all.

A friend of mine is angry at me because he says I imply on this
page that I'm Enlightened. If I'm so Enlightened, he wonders,
why do I still ask questions? Why do I still have doubts? So let me
state for the record that I am not Enlightened. Never have been
and never will be. If Enlightenment is a state without questions or
doubts, Enlightenment is the worst kind of delusion. My friend
desperately wants to enter that state beyond all doubt. Maybe you
do too.

The state without doubts or questions is the deepest Hell imagin-
able. Don't go there. It's a Buddhist's duty to keep people from
falling into such evil states.

My friend is upset because he says that I proclaim on these pages
to be Enlightened (we cleared that up, right?). Yet behind the
scenes, he says, I express doubt. What he's referring to is that last
week I sent out an e-mail to several friends detailing my ideas for
turning this web page into a book and asking for their opinions.
I wondered if such a book, an autobiography, was worth writing.
Would anyone want to read about my stupid life? If that wasn't
bad enough, when my friend sent me his opinion—which was
that my entire understanding of Buddhism was just a lot of junk
and I should give up teaching—I got kind of rattled. He's is a close
friend who I thought would understand. The worst I expected
from him was to hear my stuff was boring. I sent an e-mail to my
first Dharma teacher Tim asking his opinion of the situation and,
because I was so rattled by all this, ended up sending the e-mail
I'd intended for Tim to my friend instead. Yet more behind the
scenes doubt on my part!

My friend is now convinced I'm a complete phony.

So now I'll say it to all of you in a way none of you can possibly misinterpret:

I am a complete phony.

The only real Enlightenment is to understand that you are a complete phony. And if that sounds like me claiming Enlightenment again, I'm sorry.

If you pursue the Truth long enough there comes a time when it will wallop you upside the head. You'll have no choice but to face up to it. Get ready because it won't be what you imagined. Not even close. You may well wish you hadn't chased it so long.

It is yourself, naked and phony as all get out, all snotty and stinky.

It doesn't know a damned thing.

It has doubts and insecurities.

It gets horny sometimes and sometimes it likes to read the funny papers.

It is the source of everything in this Universe, every star, every planet, every galaxy.

It's the wellspring of all the teachings of the Great Enlightened Masters from Gautama Buddha to Dogen Zenji to your mom and dad and the guy on TV who does the pitches for Miller beer.

It is the most beautiful thing you can experience bar none.

It is God Himself.

And you cannot run away.

Once my Zen teacher, Nishijima Roshi, told me, half in jest, but not half in jest, that I understood Buddhism better than him. Do you think this made me feel elated? Like "YES! I got it!" No way. It was the most frightening thing I'd ever heard of in my life. The only thing to compare with it was the realization I had one day at work that no one in the world knew where to find the master tapes of *Ultraman: Towards the Future* if I didn't know where to find them. And I didn't have a clue where they were. Same feeling, but much bigger. If I didn't know the Truth for myself...

Once you notice all of this you have no choice but to teach it to others. Whether you're good teacher or not doesn't mean shit to the Truth. I don't have a decent forum to do so yet, so I started this web page. Once you accept Dharma Transmission you have no other choice than to teach. If you're not willing to be a big stupid looking phony just like me you'd better turn in your robes.

Mystical types like to say that we have to realize we are God. I prefer the converse.

God has to realize that He is just you and me.

AFTERWORD

Y'know, I'm not really sure who the friend referred to in this article is. I have an idea who it might be. But some of what I say in this piece couldn't possibly refer to that person. It's a mystery!

As for being a phony, I find this accusation, which I often hear, really interesting. Much of the criticism I receive about my writings seems to be directed at my not living up to what the critic in question thinks I ought to be. Therefore I am a phony. Usually this comes from people who consider themselves to have a clear understanding of what a Buddhist monk should be like. Though no actual Buddhist monks have ever made this accusation of me. It's always from people who've read a lot about monks, but never tried to live the monk's life for themselves. These folks scan books and blogs for people who live up to their expectations. And they are always disappointed.

I understand this completely and I have total sympathy. I wasted a lot of time being just like that myself. I had high ideals and scoffed at anyone who didn't live up to them. Phonies!

Of course there are a lot of people out there who set themselves up for this. They present an image of holiness and purity. But this is a dangerous game. You cannot possibly live up to someone else's ideals, no matter how exemplary you are. I feel like it's better to present yourself as a lowlife and then have people be surprised at how nice you are.

The complete story the tapes for *Ultraman: Towards The Future* that I allude to in this piece goes like this. The show in question was a 13-episode mini-series shot in Australia in the late 1980s as an attempt to break open the Western markets to Asia's top superhero, Ultraman. It failed, obviously. But the show itself wasn't half bad. At the time I wrote this article I was working for the company that made that show, though I did not work for them when the show was being produced. I was hired about three years after it was finished.

Once I got into an argument with my boss, the late Kiyotaka "Jimmy" Ugawa. We were cleaning out the warehouse of the international division where I worked and where Ugawa-san was chief. In the warehouse we found a box of tapes each of which was marked "Ultraman: Toward The Future MASTER" followed by an episode number. I said we'd better not throw these away because they were the master tapes. Ugawa-san, who had worked on the show, insisted they could not be the master tapes because only the production department had the master tapes of our shows. That was the standard procedure in the company.

I argued for a while, saying that perhaps someone had made a mistake and the tapes had ended up in our department. But I was over-ruled. Ugawa-san had worked on the show. He knew best. He made the decisions. Maybe he was right. The tapes were thrown away.

A few years later the production department came to my department asking if we knew where the master tapes of *Ultraman: Toward The Future* were. Ugawa-san claimed ignorance. Perhaps he really had forgotten. He'd handled the matter in such an off-hand way it's entirely possible he had no recollection of it. I knew where those tapes were, though.

They were at the bottom of a landfill somewhere.

The moment I refer to in this piece was the moment I realized that I really was the only one in the whole wide world who cared enough about the master tapes of *Ultraman: Toward The Future* to keep them safe. When the incident in which they were thrown away occurred I still believed that maybe there were others watching over these things. I thought that Ugawa-san might have been right. He was supposed to be an authority on the subject, after all.

This was a big moment. I had watched that show when it was first broadcast, not knowing that in a few short years I would be working for the people that made it. And now I was in charge.

It's hard to explain. But that incident seemed to reveal some really important things about taking personal responsibility. As for the master tapes of *Ultraman: Toward the Future*, eventually copies were found. But those copies had Japanese subtitles burned in that could not be removed. And to this day, all versions of the series released on video have those same subtitles.

Nothing is Sacred (Nothing is Profane)

CHAPTER 8

EXPLAINING THE UNEXPLAINABLE

INTRODUCTION

This piece is interesting to me in that I know what I was trying to say here, but I feel like I say it pretty badly. On the other hand, it generated a lot of positive response when I first put it up. So maybe I'm being too critical. How about if I let you read it yourself and then make my comments at the end?

THE ARTICLE

Practice comes first, then explanations. D'uh, right? But instead of practicing zazen and then explaining it, far too many people start with explanations and then begin a practice based on those explanations. Or worse, they dispense with practice altogether and are satisfied with explanations alone. There are a lot of very good explanations of zazen practice in Buddhist writings. But these explanations are always based on practice. Doing it any other way would be like having a guy who's never even ice-skated explain the fundamentals of hockey.

The idea of Alaya Consciousness developed by the Yogacara School is a good example of the kinds of explanations you find in Buddhist literature for the phenomena one encounters in practice. "Alaya" means "storehouse." According to this theory, every action we take "perfumes" the consciousness stream and creates a special potentiality called a "seed" which remains in our "storehouse consciousness" where it's inaccessible to conscious thought or memory. This potentiality may eventually "ripen" at which point we will find ourselves taking actions for reasons we cannot comprehend. This idea is so remarkably similar to Freud's notion of the sub-conscious it's obvious that the Yogacaran philosophers were referring to the same phenomenon. It's a phenomenon, by the way, which Western thinkers were then centuries away from coming to terms with. Because it was based on zazen practice, the idea of Alaya is deeper than those of Freud and his followers. But Freudian theory is more precise (there are fewer metaphors about seeds and perfume and so on), more rigorously tested, more widely accepted and therefore more useful to us today.

It's stupid to try and go against science. At the lectures I used to attend, the Hare Krishnas would say stuff like, "the Srimad Bhagvatam says there are people living on the Moon. Therefore, the astronauts didn't actually land on the Moon, but on another planet near by." Uh huh. When do we eat? (The Krishnas offer free dinners on Sundays, but you have to sit through a lecture first.) The 20th Century was full of religious dudes who tried to deny science. But science obviously works. It's based on the very reasonable idea that we should throw away any theory that doesn't actually work. I know this doesn't always happen. But the fact that it's supposed to work like this is very important. It's far better than the notion of holding on to out-dated theories no matter how much evidence there is against them. But if I say that too loudly who's going to give me free curry on Sunday nights?

If we want to convince people to do zazen, telling them, "Just sit there for a couple decades and you'll figure it out," doesn't have much appeal. If we rely on the traditional explanations we end up with people waiting to feel their chakras expand with Pure White Light or some other such nonsense. The idea of chakras was based on a rudimentary understanding of the human nervous system. With all their talk about energy radiating up through the spine and into the head, it's obvious those ancient Indian guys figured out there was some link between the brain and the spinal column and that sitting up straight for a long time had a beneficial effect on its workings. This is pretty amazing considering Western anatomists in those days still thought the brain was an organ for cooling the blood. Yet it's still imprecise and full of unnecessary mysticism. Why don't we do the logical thing and look at zazen in terms of the highly developed and rigorously tested theories science has developed about the central nervous system? This is much more sensible than trying to force ourselves to believe theories about the internal workings of the human body invented by people who didn't even have X-ray machines.

There hasn't been a whole lot of clinical research on zazen. Zen teachers are not well funded or scientifically minded enough (generally) to pursue such research. Those who are interested, like Gudo Nishijima, my current Zen teacher, are left to peruse the popular scientific literature looking for anything that sounds close to what they know from personal experience. This is how Nishijima came to his ideas about the human nervous system.

Nishijima believes that the body/mind dichotomy in philosophy can be explained based on the interaction of our sympathetic and para-sympathetic nervous systems. The sympathetic nervous system corresponds to "mind" and the parasympathetic to "body." The sympathetic nervous system deals with what we normally call mental functioning, both conscious and subconscious. It's what goes on in your head, in those parts of your brain devoted to what some call higher functioning. The parasympathetic nervous system deals with more bodily oriented matters. This is the stuff that happens mostly in your lower brain and in your spinal cord. When the sympathetic nervous system is stronger we're more "spiritual" and when the parasympathetic nervous system is stronger we're more "materialistic." That electrochemical energy we call thought is generated by both halves of the nervous system even though conscious thought is perceived by the sympathetic nervous system.

In addition, there are electrochemical interactions going on in your brain all the time which researchers call "near field" and "far field." When you're more alert and active, there's lots of "near field" activity going on. People in lower states of awareness, such as coma, generate very little "near field" brain activity. To use Nishijima's terminology, it may be that "near field" activity is more "spiritual" and "far field" activity more "materialistic." The difference we suppose exists between body and mind occurs to us only because our nervous system is out of balance.

The separation of the two nervous systems is an illusion. They interact with each other all the time. There is nothing we could call the seat of consciousness. Consciousness extends throughout the body. And farther. Someone who's done a lot of zazen might tell you that his or her brain extends all the way to the ends of the Universe. We'll leave that aside for now. But please don't forget it. If you think this stuff is too dry and mechanical, go back three sentences and read again.

So why do we need to know all this stuff? Well, we don't really need to know. But it helps to know. The older explanations of how zazen worked were not only imprecise, they're also bound up with a lot of cultural stuff we really can't relate to anymore. There are Buddhist texts that talk about fire and wind as elements. We wouldn't call these things elements anymore. Most Buddhist practitioners understand this as just an ancient way of describing the world and take it as such. Yet when we read about things like Alaya Consciousness and so on, we tend to think the texts are talking about something mystical. They're not. The writers of the Buddhist Sutras (the good ones anyway) were never trying to describe something mystical or strange. They were trying to describe their real experience in this world.

People hearing this kind of an explanation may be left cold, thinking that if they accept it it, there's no fun in life anymore, no mystery. They think they know all about this world and that mystery only exists in the great "Somewhere Else." But scientific stuff is very mysterious. We can explain how gravity works. But why is there gravity at all? This is very mysterious, very mystical. People talk about the "mundane world." But there's nothing mundane at all about the world we live in. It's constantly amazing. I used to wonder why Zen guys wore such drab clothes and lived in such dull looking places. It's because to them even those clothes and those places are as vibrant and exciting as Saturday night on the Vegas strip.

Mind and body are one. Zazen is as much a physical exercise as it is a mental process. This is what clearly distinguishes it from "meditation" as the word is usually understood, as well as from such purely mental processes as self-hypnosis. Western writers, along with far too many zazen practitioners, get this all bass-ack-wards. They suppose that we take the physical posture of zazen in order to work on some kind of mental exercise. But zazen is no more a mental exercise than jogging or tennis. Athletes know that certain mental effects flow from the practice of exercise and sports. It's the same with zazen. In fact, athletic and artistic activities often give rise to the same kind of mental balance as zazen. The big difference is that you finish zazen feeling less tired than when you started.

Religions and regular philosophies only appeal to the sympathetic nervous system. They're just in our heads. Buddhism is something completely different, a philosophy that includes both body and mind.

AFTERWORD

When I tried to put some of Nishijima's theories about the sympathetic and parasympathetic nervous systems into my first book, Hardcore Zen, my editor refused to let them pass. I was not a medical doctor, he said, nor did I have any kind of degree in neuroscience. I was therefore unqualified to say anything at all about the human nervous system.

I was completely baffled by this attitude, and remain baffled by it to this day. Yet I have to concede that in a sense my editor was correct. He was incorrect in saying that only people with recognized qualifications could comment on these matters. But he was correct in realizing that most people believe that only experts may address these matters. He was right to take it out of the book. It would have hurt sales. And it was his job to make a sellable book.

I'm not sure why the perception exists that only medical experts may address matters of the human nervous system. It's like saying only an astronomy professor can talk about the solar system. The theory of the human nervous system is part of our common Western understanding of ourselves. The theory is simple enough that most of us understand its basics even if we don't grasp all the nuances. We don't really need to be experts in order to be qualified to talk about it at least in very general terms. And this is what Nishijima did.

Nishijima read books on the human nervous system and he understood the basics of the theory of how it works. He found in these books a way of explaining the effects he felt from zazen practice in contemporary terms. He was grateful for the opportunity to free zazen up from the mystical sounding terminology it had previously relied upon. He wasn't trying to advance a new theory about how the human nervous system operates. He was trying to use what was known about the human nervous system to express what happens in zazen practice.

What I am trying to do in this piece is to use Nishijima's theories to reflect upon my own real experiences in Zen practice and explain those experiences in terms of what I know about the human nervous system. This is exactly what ancient meditators attempted to do when they talked about charkas and the movement of energy and so forth. Most of them probably weren't experts on those matters either. They were simply using the then-current understanding of physiology to explain their real experience in words that their contemporaries could understand and relate to. That's what Nishijima was trying to do when he talked about the human nervous system.

I have to say that initially I resisted Nishijima's explanations. I felt that by reducing everything to the workings of the nervous system we would lose the beauty and wonder of the unknown and unknowable. But I was wrong. Just because we call something the human nervous system doesn't mean we really understand what it is. It just means we have a name for it. The human nervous system itself is a very mystical thing. The fact that it exists at all is a kind of miracle. We take these kinds of miracles for granted. And that's a real shame.

CHAPTER 9

MATTERS OF BELIEF

INTRODUCTION

This piece seems pretty straight forward to me. I'm not sure how much of an introduction is needed. Emily is still a friend of mine. She has two kids now. She used to say that if she ever had a child, she would name it Palak Paneer. Some time later she had twins. She did not name either of them Palak Paneer. I was highly disappointed.

THE ARTICLE

I got an e-mail this week from my friend Emily. It seems she's been getting interested in Christianity. The problem is she doesn't believe in Jesus.

Personally, whenever I hear people talk about "believing in Jesus" or Krishna or The Great Mother Spirit or America or what have you, I have no idea what that's supposed to mean.

I once had a discussion with a Christian guy who seemed to think that if a person believed Jesus actually literally did all the things he's supposed to have done, that person would be scared of Jesus' power and would therefore be converted. This is a pretty simpleminded view and it's certainly not the one held by all Christians. But hearing it showed me the limitations of that kind of literal belief in the historical accuracy of various ancient texts.

If you're not scared by it, then does it really matter whether something miraculous did or didn't actually happen in some obscure country several thousand years ago (I include the miraculous stories about Buddha here too, by the way)? History is certainly relevant. I majored in history in college. But it doesn't make a sensible basis for belief. Christianity hasn't made much headway in India because stories of guys who walk on water, raise the dead and heal the sick are so common there that those parts of the New Testament is hardly surprising to anyone. "He walked on water? There's a guy over in the next village who does that too!" By the same token, it doesn't impress many of us in the West anymore because we've learned how thoroughly even very recent history can be distorted.

I've always thought that if Christianity (or any other religion) is true, it is just as true even if someone proves beyond all doubt that Jesus (or whatever deity or prophet) never really existed. There are a lot of Buddhist sutras with words attributed to Gautama Buddha, which everyone knows were written centuries after the man died. Yet most Buddhists are perfectly comfortable with this apparent contradiction.

Buddha is something more than the historical person. Buddha is that part of any human being which apprehends the truth. So whoever wrote that stuff, if it's true, Buddha really did write it. It goes further. Those Sutras (the true ones, at least), though they were written hundreds of years after Gautama died and though Gautama is not sitting up in Heaven making other people write stuff in his name, were actually written by the historical person Gautama Buddha. If this seems absurd, it's because our usual understanding of what constitutes a "person" is mistaken. If "believing in Jesus" is something similar to that, then I believe in Jesus.

You need both doubt and faith. Faith keeps you going forward. Doubt keeps you from going forward with a blindfold on. You don't need to resolve the contradiction between the two, to try to become completely faithful or to doubt everything. In fact, you should not try to resolve it because you'll fail anyway. "There is no God and He is your creator" is an old Buddhist saying. I've always liked that one.

Everybody's faith is different. One of the great myths in religious groups is the one that says that everyone within a given group believes the same thing. That isn't even possible. The mere fact of being a human being with your own brain rules out the possibility you could think exactly the same way as anyone else.

In Buddhism the object of belief is reality itself, this world, our own lives. That might seem weird. How can someone "believe in reality?" But most of us don't believe in the reality we experience every moment of every day. That's why we're always trying to escape into religious beliefs, or into physical pleasures or into the kind of mindless zoned out state induced by video games and endless web surfing. There are as many escapes as there are people. Many more, in fact.

To really believe in reality requires tremendous effort. The biggest problem is that most of us think we understand reality pretty well already. Our frustrations in life occur when the reality we experience doesn't match up with the image of reality we carry around in our heads. Rather than modifying what's in our brains we fight against reality and try to change it instead. Or, if we do modify what's in our heads, that modification becomes rigid and when something comes along that doesn't match up with the new version we're back to fighting it again. What's in our heads will never exactly match up with reality.

So does that mean we just don't know squat? That no one knows squat? That "enlightenment" is just acknowledging you don't know anything at all? That's part of it, yes. But I'm afraid it's far too easy to just stop there. I'm not going to let you off with that one. The fact is you know so much squat you are (like me and everyone else) deeply terrified to face up to what you know, to face what you really are. That's very hard to do. And that's what believing in reality is all about. If you see good in the world, you see it because of what's good in you. If you see evil, it's because of your own capacity for evil. If you try and ignore that, pretend it doesn't exist, you'll go terribly wrong. But if you give in to it, the consequences may be even worse. Good and evil are just ideas, thoughts.

What we think is just the functioning of our brain cells. It's not reality. What we perceive is just the stimuli from our sense organs. So we can't call that "reality" either. But although we can't perceive reality, nor can we think about reality, it may be that reality can perceive us and even think about us. And reality knows all kinds of squat. Reality is more you than you could ever be. Thought isn't reality. But it can be a mirror of reality if our body and mind is balanced. A good mirror can only show a part of the sky. But it shows it with perfect clarity. Though good and evil are just ideas, we should always strive to do good and avoid evil.

We think that we're struggling now, but if only we could reach whatever goal we've set for ourselves—"Enlightenment," perhaps—we'd end up in a place where we don't have to struggle. In truth, you were born into this world for only one reason. You had a deep desire to struggle in exactly the way you are struggling right this very minute. To finish struggling is to finish living. Life never really ends, though, because it never really began. Ideas about Heaven or simplistic ideas about Enlightenment are absurd because they attempt to picture life without struggle. It's like trying to picture a live fish without envisioning water. Ain't no such thing!

Buddhism is sometimes thought of as atheistic. But it's not at all.

Buddhists believe in God. God is the Universe and the Universe is God. Reality is God. Reality is the object of Buddhist belief and Buddhist worship. It's God because the sum total of everything that is or ever was or ever will be can't be anything else.

Divinity isn't something special, something reserved for great people in ancient books or imaginary beings who live far, far away and watch over us from a safe distance. Divinity is everywhere. There really isn't anything that's not divine. That's what Jesus' message was.

The people who killed him did so as a way to prove him wrong. How could they be divine if they could do such a horrible and stupid thing? But he proved them wrong by saying that even that action was part of the divine plan.

AFTERWORD

At the time I wrote this I was very fond of using Nishijima's formula for verbal pronouncements that began "Buddhist believe in." I soon discovered that these pronouncements often made certain people mad. These people considered themselves Buddhists and they didn't believe in those things. They didn't like me acting as a spokesman for them. So I dropped the "Buddhists believe in" statements.

Along those lines, my statement that "most Buddhists are perfectly comfortable with this apparent contradiction (of sutras that were written after Gautama's death but purport to be his words)" would be challenged by a lot of people. It's the Mahayana Buddhists who take this position. And statistically they're the majority. So the statement isn't technically wrong. But adherents of Theravada Buddhism do not accept these later sutras.

I still contend that Buddhists believe in God. I think lots of Buddhists are highly uncomfortable with the word God. Some are so uncomfortable with the word that they insist they don't believe in God. That's fine. I still think they do believe.

Most scholars seem to agree that it's a mistake to call Buddhism atheistic. It's better to call it non-theistic. I'm not comfortable with the word agnostic either. The word agnostic, it seems to to me, usually is used to refer to a slightly wishy-washy position. An agnostic, as far as I can determine, doesn't know whether to believe in God or not and therefore takes no position one way or the other. I don't feel like Buddhism takes no position on the matter of God.

Buddhism proceeds from the position that there is an ultimate ground of all being and non-being. It proceeds from the position that our experience of the universe is a real and integral part of the universe. It's not that we just happen to be conscious of the universe. Our consciousness of the universe is a fundamental component of the universe. It can't be subtracted from the rest of the universe.

Although having said that, I would also hasten to point out that it is not the Buddhist way to insist that all Buddhists must believe that. You could be an agnostic Buddhist or an atheist Buddhist or even a Muslim or Christian Buddhist.

In any case, to me, this understanding of the nature of things is, I think, contained within all of the canonical Buddhist literature. It suggests what I would call a belief in God. It's not an unfounded belief in a supernatural super being. There is nothing supernatural about God. Although our understanding of what is natural is woefully incomplete. The Buddhist understanding of God is not based on speculation but upon observation of our real experience. I'm writing a whole other book on this subject in which I'll probably repeat the foregoing paragraphs. So I'll leave the discussion there for now.

The rest of this piece seems to me to be yet another example of me rejecting the idea that there is a mundane reality that we can ignore in favor of focusing our attention on some imagined "higher" reality. I think it's really important to absolutely believe in the reality we live in at this moment. And I still find that difficult sometimes, at least intellectually. The mind is always trying to run off in some other direction. So we have to watch it constantly.

That's what zazen practice is for. Why not try it sometime and see for yourself?

CHAPTER 10

PAST LIFE REGRESSION?

INTRODUCTION

My dad no longer practices hypnotism professionally. That's a shame, I think. He was apparently really good at getting people to stop smoking.

THE ARTICLE

So my dad, the soon-to-be-professional hypnotist, keeps asking me about past life regressions. What do I think of the idea? What's the Buddhist view on that kind of stuff? Should he try one (a friend in his hypno class has offered to regress him)? I've tried to come up with a good answer. But the issue is too complex to try and compress between the usual "How's the dog?" "What did you say, mom? Dad was talking over you" and "What's grandma worried about this week?" of our trans-Pacific telephone conversations. I thought my answer might make an OK installment of this page. Here goes.

I think if someone wants to try a past life regression, they ought to try it. But I'd advise that person to be very skeptical about what he or she experiences.

When Buddha was asked about past lives, future births, life after death and so on his answer was, "The question does not fit the case." (Some texts say he was silent, but I prefer this answer).

When people ask Nishijima Roshi, my teacher, about life after
death he is very adamant that true Buddhism denies both life
after death and reincarnation. "This is a very important point," he
usually adds.

Of course, there are plenty of Buddhist teachers who'll tell you
different. Certain Buddhists, mostly from Tibetan traditions,
seem to have based most of their teachings on ideas about life
after death and reincarnation. Philip Kapleau wrote a book in
which he tried to explain why the Zen idea of rebirth is different from the usual idea of reincarnation. Though his ideas are
well presented and very logical, the book still misses the point by
miles. The best answer to the question goes like this:

A guy walks up to a Zen Master and asks, "Is there life after
death?"

The Zen Master says, "How should I know?"

The guy's face goes red, veins pop out of his forehead and he yells,
"Cuz you're a Zen Master!"

"Yes," says the Zen Master, "but I'm not a dead one."

When you ask about life after death you are already assuming
you know all there is to know about life during life. But do you?
Which is more important to you?

I went to Shanghai three years ago. If you ask me what Shanghai
is like, I can describe a few things I remember about the place
and you can picture those things in your mind. But my memories of Shanghai aren't 100% reliable. Ask my wife who was there
with me and she might describe things pretty differently. What's
more, the mental pictures you will create based on my rather iffy
information will be pieced together from your own memories of

places you've been, none of which are Shanghai (let's assume, for this discussion, none of you has ever been there). And above and beyond all of that Shanghai has changed a lot in the past three years. Much of what I'll describe to you about the place isn't true anymore.

When it comes to memories of past lives, we're in a much more vague area. Hell, I can't even say with complete clarity what happened in my life this morning. Even if there really is some mechanism by which I can access memories of things that happened before my birth as a Zen Master, rock and roll idol and bit player in Ultraman movies, I would be very suspicious of those memories.

Memory is something no one really understands very well. The old idea that our brain is kind of tape recorder that can play back the things that happened to us with perfect reliability has been repeatedly proven false. There may be deeper memory traces in our own brains that we aren't aware of. I've read that all human beings are born with a fear of heights and a fear of snakes. How they test this, I do not want to know. Our pre-human ancestors who feared these things tended to avoid them and thereby lived long enough to pass on their genes and their fears to subsequent generations. That human beings were able to evolve at all is partially due to this effect. This kind of mental hard wiring could be seen as a type of memory. Since the human brain is a very complex thing, there are certainly other far more subtle "memories" of this kind wired into it through the course of evolution. Jung's idea of "racial memories" could be true. People will tend to experience these "memories" in idiosyncratic ways and the very real feeling of these mental traces being parts of previous lives could result.

Or they could be real past life memories.

How should I know?

The point is that whole life after death thing is terribly seductive. And it's dangerous too. Our friend Mohamet Atta (the purported leader of the attacks on New York on September 11, 2001) couldn't have completed his deadly mission if he hadn't believed he'd be rewarded after he died. I, for one, often hope there is an afterlife so that people like him can spend eternity with their testicles being smashed by sledgehammers against red hot anvils. You can get hooked on after-life ideas just like a drug. The reason to avoid ideas about life after death isn't because they couldn't possibly be true. It's because these ideas can never really be accurate. They promote a kind of dreamy fantasy state that distracts us from seeing what our life is right now.

It's also because the question doesn't fit the case. Life after death is not what we are experiencing right here and right now. Or, if you really want to believe in reincarnation, then this is life after death. Do you think you understand it? I once knew a person who said she didn't need to practice Zazen because she was certain that after she died all would be revealed. So why bother trying to figure it out now? Zazen isn't about trying to see what will happen after you die. It's about seeing clearly what your real life is right now.

Notice how the only way we can believe in any description of the afterlife is if it comes from some kind of mystical source—something drastically removed from our real lives. It has to be based on some terribly ancient book, on the words of some venerable old guru, on the testimony of people who've "crossed over to the other side" and returned to tell the tale. I'm safe from being asked about such matters. Look at my picture on the top page of this website and ask yourself if anybody in their right mind would believe that guy's ideas about life after death (the photo was of me dressed in a monster costume). The things we believe about life after death are never based on our real experience right now. Even if you've personally survived a near death experience or have gone through a past life regression, the important question is: Where is that experience now? It's floating around in your head somewhere. But it's not real.

Our past is never real, no matter whether it happened 600 years ago when you were Leopold the Bold scaling the Himalayas on a camel or whether it happened six minutes ago when you were fishing a large and pleasingly aesthetically shaped booger out of your nose. The past is always memory. Cause and effect are real. What we did in the past has bearing on our present and future. But no matter how clear our memory may be of any particular event, we can't really say we understand the past because we can't go back there. The mind of the past is unknowable. The mind of the future is unknowable. The mind of the present is unknowable. Do you really think you completely understand what's going on right now? Honestly? By the time you can examine any moment with what we call objectivity, that moment is dead and gone and everything has changed. And everything keeps right on changing as we attempt to freeze some piece of our past so we can look at it clearly without it wriggling around like a centipede caught in a pair of tweezers held in a very shaky hand.

I wouldn't go seeking out a past life regression for myself. But if my dad offered to regress me, I might just be tempted to try it once (depending on what he charges). I'm very wary of "altered states of consciousness" in general, though, and the idea of being hypnotized bothers me a bit (this is also why I don't drink). At any rate, I wouldn't say "no" to the possibility something authentic and useful could happen in such a situation. But I wouldn't get hooked on the experience. I wouldn't build my life around it. I wouldn't trust that my memories from past lives, should I come across any, are any more accurate than my memories of my own childhood or my memories of where I stored the many important files I'm supposed to take care of at work (where are those things, anyway). Nor would I trust that what appear to be past life memories really are exactly what they seem. If past life regressions are viewed this way and those who undergo them are mentally stable there may be no more harm in them than there is in going to see a movie or reading a really neat book. I think an honest hypnotist should avoid offering past life regressions. But if a client who the hypnotist knows to be a mentally stable person wants one and if the hypnotist refrains from making unbelievable claims about it, it's not such a terrible thing to do. It might even be fun.

AFTERWORD

I still stand by what I wrote here. I tend to be a little gentler with people who ask about reincarnation than Nishijima Roshi was. He was never actually mean about it. But he was absolutely set against the idea and would not mince words. I, on the other hand, mince.

I'm not sure what happens after we die. But I think that as soon as we frame the question in terms of "after we die" we're already looking in the wrong place for the answer. We die every nanosecond of every day. To imagine that there's a different kind of death awaiting us in the future is a mistake, I think.

On the other hand, there will come a time when there will be no Brad Warner that you can write to and complain about this book. I won't come back. And yet I feel that there is some kind of continuity. What I think of as Brad Warner is a manifestation of the universe. And the universe is eternal. Still, I don't like to speculate any further than that. It's useless to do so.

Dogen was a staunch opponent of the belief in reincarnation. There are a number of places in Shobogenzo where he characterizes reincarnation as a "non-Buddhist belief." He usually calls it something like "the non-Buddhist philosophy of Senika." Senika was a Brahmanist (often called Hindu these days) philosopher who believed that the body was transitory but that the soul was immortal.

On the other hand, Dogen also insists that the mind is mountains, rivers and the earth. So our consciousness is not limited in the ways we usually imagine. But, having said this, he also says in his Shobogenzo essay "Mind Here and Now is Buddha" that, "mind as mountains, rivers and the earth is nothing other than mountains, rivers and the earth." We are not something other than what we are.

As far as past life regressions are concerned, I remain highly skeptical. Every time I meet someone who believes they're remembered a past life I just end up rolling my eyes. I met this guy recently who claimed to have been an Aztec warrior a few hundred years ago. Now he was an overweight red headed super nerd. I could tell he was really excited about his past life. And his excitement made me even more dubious of his story. His past life seemed much more real to him than his current one.

I've never done a past life regression myself. But I still think it might be fun. It's just not something I'm inclined to work at very hard. I'm curious to see if I would come up with any memories. I wonder what they might be and if I'd believe them. I tend not to believe everything I remember about my current life. So I'm not sure how much stock I'd put in memories of lives before this one.

CHAPTER 11

REINCARNATION AND ALL THAT

INTRODUCTION

Here's another piece about reincarnation. Parts of this were used in *Hardcore Zen*. I'll say more about it at the end.

THE ARTICLE

Last week I attended the annual 3-day Zazen retreat hosted by Nishijima Sensei at Tokei-in temple in the tea covered hills of Shizuoka (2 hrs. from Tokyo by Bullet Train). As usual, the question of reincarnation came up during the talks. And, as usual, Nishijima expressed his opinion that there was no such thing as reincarnation and that the belief in reincarnation is not Buddhism. And, like always, most of the people who heard this were pretty cheesed off about it. After all, everybody knows that all Buddhists believe in reincarnation. Richard Gere says so!

I'm not trying to sound high and mighty here. Seven years ago when I began studying with Nishijima, I too asked the reincarnation question and I too was pretty cheesed off by his reply. I should have known better, really. After all, I'd been practicing for a decade or so by then. It's not hard for me to understand why people ask the question. We're all scared of dying and we all want some kind of assurance that we're going to live forever. Having a kindly old man in black robes tell you you're going to be reborn after you die is pretty comforting.

When Gautama Buddha was asked about life after death, eternal existence and so on, he said "the question does not fit the case." The question can't be answered because it's the wrong question. In the chapter titled *Bendowa* in Shobogenzo, Dogen, the founder of the Soto school of Zen in Japan, says this about reincarnation. "According to that non-Buddhist view, there is one spiritual intelligence existing within our body. When this body dies, however, the spirit casts off the skin and is reborn. If we learn this view as the Buddha's Dharma we are even more foolish than the person who grasps a tile or pebble thinking it to be a golden treasure." (from the translation by Gudo Nishijima and Chodo Cross, Windbell 1994)Some might say that what Dogen is talking about here is transmigration and that reincarnation is a different idea. But the two terms are so entangled these days that the difference really doesn't matter much. What's more, the Shobogenzo is just chock full of stories of people dying here and being reborn somewhere else as a different person. What gives?

You know what? Quoting quotes and reading books will not solve the problem. If I just quoted Dogen and left it at that I'd be like one of those guys with the bumper stickers that say "The Bible said it, I believe it and that settles it." Either understand things for yourself or shut the hell up. I'll give you my take on the matter and let you sort it out on your own.

Our brain likes to label things. That's its job. In our minds there is something we call "me." This "me" consists of all of our memories, dreams for the future, likes and dislikes and so on. But "me" is also our label for something ineffable, something we cannot understand or put into words. In moments of balance and clarity, we can see that this "me" does not belong to us at all. It is the possession of the Universe. It is the the Universe itself. My first teacher, Tim, used to say "It's more you than you could ever be." Nishijima says "my personality extends throughout the Universe." This something is the same as the present moment. The present moment is eternal. It's always there. It is unborn and it cannot die. But it's not "me" and it does not reincarnate.

If we watch a river flow, we can see bubbles form on its surface. The bubbles appear, float along for a while, then burst. The bubbles are just air and water. The water returns to the river. The air returns to the atmosphere. But that bubble will never appear again. If we light a candle, then use the flame to light a second candle while simultaneously blowing out the first, is the flame on the second candle the same flame as the first? Where is the first flame? Snap your fingers. Where was that sound before you heard it? After you heard it, where did it go?

When we die, we die. We never appear again. But why should this worry us so much? We die all the time. Every moment of every day we die. Look at a picture of yourself when you were 10 years old. Where is that person now? If we look all over the world, if we scour the Universe, we will not find that person. He is gone and no one will ever see him again. Each moment is our life. Here and now is our life. We want to live forever, we want to be reincarnated, because we have a confused idea of who we are. The "me" we want to live forever can never do so because this "me" does not exist. It is not a thing which can possibly live forever. It is always changing. We don't have to worry about it dying, because it's already dead and gone. In fact, change is so constant, so all-pervasive that we have to question the very idea we call "change." Nothing changes because our concept of "change" implies that some kind of permanent substance makes itself into different forms and yet in its essence remains consistent. There is no essence.

Forget about reincarnation. Look at your life as it is right now and live it.

AFTERWORD

I'm not sure there's much else to say. As I get older the idea of life after death gets more and more appealing. I think this happens to a lot of people. There have been plenty of cases where folks who staunchly denied life after death changed their mind later in life. The reason is obvious.

But it's still a matter of the question not fitting the case. Asking if there is life after death means you're already thinking of life in a very particular way. You think that you exist as a single entity moving through time. You wonder if this entity will continue after the death of your body.

But time and you are bound together. Who you are now isn't an older version of the same you that you were ten years ago. Who you are now is a manifestation of this moment. It has a strong relationship with who you were ten years ago. But it's not the same thing at all. You in the future will be a manifestation of the future.

The idea that the real you is this thing that lives inside your body and pops out at the moment of death is to absurd to address. I know a lot of people believe it anyway. But it really makes no sense.

The idea that the personal self survives the death of the body is also iffy. No one can really say for certain it doesn't. But all the supposed evidence I've seen that it does is fairly dubious. Did the Dalai Lama really recognize the toothbrush he used in his previous incarnation? Actually I don't know if a toothbrush was involved, but they do customarily test the babies they decide might be reincarnated Lamas objects used by their supposed former selves in order to test them. I'm extremely skeptical.

Yet I feel that whatever it is that we are is fundamental to the universe. As I quoted Tim McCarthy saying in the second chapter of this book, " You couldn't exist without the whole of the Universe being just as it is and the whole of the Universe couldn't exist without you."

I just think that the concept reincarnation is a very poor model of what happens. Kosho Uchiyama said, "Life is not born because a person is born. The life of the whole Universe has been ladled into the hardened idea called 'I'. Life does not disappear because a person dies. Simply, the life of the whole Universe has been poured out of this hardened idea of 'I' back into the Universe."

CHAPTER 12

ONE IS THE LONELIEST NUMBER

INTRODUCTION

Kobun Chino Roshi was my first Zen teacher's teacher. I never met the man himself. But I feel that a lot of what he was reached me through my teacher, Tim McCarthy. When he died suddenly in 2002 I was shocked and saddened. I wrote this piece shortly after he died.

THE ARTICLE

In honor of the life work of Kobun Chino, I thought I'd take up something that he said in one of his lectures. I hope that any of Kobun's students who might be reading this can forgive me for being so presumptuous as to comment upon his words. But I feel he was one of the truest Zen teachers around and I think it's worth looking closely at some of what he said. I can't improve upon his words, but I can tell you what they mean to me.

Kobun said, "Wanting to be alone is impossible. When you become really alone you notice you are not alone. In other words, we stop our vigorous efforts towards ideal purity. Purity is just a process. After purity, dry simplicity comes, where almost no more life is there, and your sensation is that you are not existing any more. Still, you are existing there. You flip into the other side of nothing, where you discover everybody is waiting for you. Before that, you are living together like that—day, sun, moon, stars, and food—everything is helping you, but you are all blocked off, a closed system. You just see things from inside toward the outside, and act with incredible, systematic, logical dynamics, and you think everything is all right. When noise, or chaotic situations come, you want to leave that situation to be alone. But there is no such aloneness!

"It is very important to experience the complete negation of yourself, which brings you to the other side of nothing. People experience that in many ways. You go to the other side of nothing, and you are held by the hand of the absolute. You see yourself as part of the absolute, so you have no more insistence of self as yourself. You can speak of self as no-self upon the absolute. Only real existence is absolute."

This is great stuff. Until I read this I had been puzzled by a phrase that comes up over and over in Shobogenzo. Dogen always refers to things which are experienced by "Buddhas alone together with Buddhas." It sounds like nonsense. But it isn't.

The idea that you can be alone is an illusion. It never happens. When you're alone in your room, your room is there with you. When you're sent down to solitary confinement in a tiny little prison cell, your cell is your friend. This isn't just poetry. This is concrete fact. In Kobun's words, "you stop (your) vigorous efforts towards ideal purity." It takes a great deal of effort to sustain the illusion that you are something eternally separate from the rest of the Universe. But you've made this kind of effort for so long and worked so hard at it that it's become a habit, an addiction. Like any addict, you stick with the idea that you absolutely need your fix in the face of a mountain of evidence to the contrary. In spite of the intense pain and suffering the idea of self generates, you never want to give it up. You've convinced yourself that the alternative will kill you. In fact it will kill the idea of who you are by revealing who you actually are. It hurts to give up any addiction. Even though you know it's better to live without whatever you've become addicted to, you still have a strong desire for more poison.

The mistaken idea that we're eternally separate from everything else makes us postulate the idea of a God who can also be separate from His creations. But God is right here. "Right here" is what some Buddhists call God.

Nothing you do is ever really just for yourself. Everything you do has consequences which will affect other people and other things. That's why you always have to be very careful. At the same time it's vital that you do act. You can't get paralyzed trying to predict the possible effects of your actions. Do what's right moment by moment and the outcome will take care of itself.

You cannot be alone because you are always surrounded by you. You extend all the way out beyond the farthest stars. And you are as intimate as the air that embraces you and slips its way inside your body. There's nothing here but you. Yet you're never alone. "You go to the other side of nothing, and you are held by the hand of the absolute." When you're nothing, you are everything. I'm not just trying to be cute here. It's really true. You experience all of creation from right here. A God who remained separate from His creations could never experience the magical wonder that is you finding the carcass of a weird green insect under your sink and wondering how to get it out of there without touching it with your bare hands. What a sad creature God must be...

Sometimes Buddhism sounds like solipsism, the idea that you're the only real thing in the Universe. But that's not it. It's not that you alone are real. Everything—including you—is equally real, and equally unreal. Only our unbalanced thinking can come up with the absurd idea that there is any difference between ourselves and the whole of creation and call one real and the other false. It's all you and it's all me and we can face each other. When we face each other honestly, there is never any reason to compete, to fight, to cause each other any kind of harm. The whole idea is perfectly silly. Laughable.

But before you can face another person honestly, you have to face yourself honestly. And that's hard. That's why practice is needed.

AFTERWORD

And there you have my best effort at explaining what I mean when I use the word God. I suppose it just sounds like the ramblings of an acid head to most people. But there ya go anyway.

One Is The Loneliest Number

CHAPTER 13

THERE'S NO FUTURE FOR YOU!

INTRODUCTION

This one is a little slice-of-life from my time sitting listening to Nishijima Roshi's talks at the Young Buddhists Association of Tokyo University every Saturday afternoon.

Some time in the 1980's, Gudo Nishijima Roshi started giving lectures in English on Zen Buddhism at his home in Chiba, a depressing industrial suburb of Tokyo, to a small group of foreign students. After a couple of years, Nishijima called up Tokyo University, the school he had graduated from, and arranged to use a room there provided by the university's Young Buddhists Association. His group met there every Saturday at 1 pm for half an hour of zazen practice followed by an hour of lecture and discussion.

I started attending these sessions in 1994, the year I moved to Tokyo to work at Tsuburaya Productions, the film and TV production company who made Ultraman. It was a small group of around seven or eight people most weeks. I can't recall there ever being more than 15 people present. The lectures would normally begin with Nishijima Roshi reading a passage from his translation of Dogen's Shobogenzo, sometimes stopping to explain what he was reading, but often just reading straight through. This would go on for around 20-30 minutes after which he'd take questions.

Depending on who was there, the Q&A sessions could get quite heated. Nishijima had a very forthright manner that could rub certain people the wrong way. They seemed to take it as an invitation to challenge him. Nishijima never shied away from these challenges. I got the impression he liked a good fight. He could sometimes seem inflexible. But I don't think that was the case.

The scene I describe in the following piece is a good example. I'm certain that the person I call Mr. Spectrum here thought of Nishijima as being ridiculously set in his ways. But that wasn't the impression I got. Mr. Spectrum was presenting Nishijima with anger and confusion translated into vague speculations about the nature of things. Nishijima rejected this.

THE ARTICLE

Last week a guy came to Nishijima Roshi's weekly lecture and started up a discussion—OK, let's be honest here—an argument that I found really fascinating. The man was very perturbed about Nishijima's insistence that scientific progress was a wonderful thing. Nishijima believes that scientific ideas about the function of the autonomic nervous system have finally given us a clear and reliable understanding of just how Zazen works in the physical sense. For 2,500 years, practitioners have known that Zazen works, but until the 20th century no one could say just how or why. Nishijima is particularly fond of pointing out findings concerning the opposing forces of the sympathetic and parasympathetic nervous systems which he feels is a very useful way to explain Buddhist philosophy in a concrete way.

The guy objected. Science is far too limited. He said that the Chinese had discovered the existence of two opposing forces centuries ago and had called them Yin and Yang, that the Buddhists had discovered the realms of the subconscious ages before psychology came into existence and so on. Nishijima agreed that this was true, but said that before science came along it was all very vague and insubstantial. This didn't satisfy the guy who got very upset that a lowly "materialistic" explanation was being applied to lofty spiritual concepts. "The material world," he said "is just one manifestation of the Limitless Spectrum of Mind!"

"That is not Buddhism," Nishijima replied. "If you want to believe in something like that there is no reason for you to study Buddhism."

Here's another story. Once my previous Zen teacher, Tim McCarthy, was with his teacher Kobun Chino while Kobun was giving a talk about Zen. Someone asked Kobun about flying saucers. Kobun told him, "You should ask Tim about that. He reads comic books!"
And an observation; most of the people I know through my Zen stuff are absolutely horrified by my love of trashy rock music and bad monster movies (particularly Godzilla) and absolutely mortified that I work for a company which specializes in making whack-o science fiction films. The more "advanced" these Zen guys consider themselves, the more they pity me for being involved in such lowly things.

Of course, the idea that the Material World is but one manifestation in the Infinite Spectrum of Mind is deep philosophy. Flying saucers and Godzilla, that's just kids' stuff.

Sorry. But I don't think so.

It wasn't so long ago that I was like that guy at Nishijima's lecture—let's call him "Mr. Spectrum," shall we? In fact I admire his bravery in even bringing it up. I used to just let those same thoughts smolder in my brain. I sensed that something was wrong and that if I did bring those pretty dreams to light they'd get smashed flat like Christmas ornaments under a ball peen hammer.

Zen insists on the absolute oneness of body and mind, or matter and spirit. This can be a tough idea to swallow. In fact I suspect that anyone who doesn't find this idea hard to stomach hasn't quite come to grips with what it means. When Nishijima is asked about life after death he likes to answer that since body and mind are one, when his body dies his mind will too and that will be the end of it. If you don't have a tough time with that little nugget, you're far too spiritually advanced to be reading this page. Another thing he likes to say is "Consciousness is just an idea." Chew on that for a while.

Like Mr. Spectrum, most of us long to believe in Somewhere Else. The mystically inclined imagine Somewhere Else as the various other manifestations of the Infinite Spectrum of Mind. More "down-to-Earth" types imagine Somewhere Else as the day when they'll be filthy rich with all the babes (or dudes, or horses, what-have-you) they can handle. For frustrated regular folks Somewhere Else is all the fun those rich people, or those popular people, or those beautiful people are having right now that they will never be able to experience (smolder). Maybe Somewhere Else is the lost days of our youth when we were so much happier than we are now (people who believe this should try talking to real children some time). It could be the Paradise we'll live in after we die. It could be all the happiness we'd have if only we could get the very last stamp for our collection. Just like Mr. Spectrum's infinite spectrum of Mind, there are infinite different versions of the Great Somewhere Else. You have your Somewhere Else, too. So do I. They're all far, far away and they always will be.

There is no Somewhere Else. There's no Heaven. There's no better life ahead. As Johnny Rotten said, "There's noooo future for you!"

Pretty nihilistic, isn't it? Put it that way and this Zen thing sounds horrible, gloomy and awful. Yet the philosophy in which there is no Heaven and things will never get better for you is the brightest, most optimistic philosophy there ever was.

How can that be when we're living in the rottenest, most polluted, on-the-brink-of-WWIII world there ever was? George Harrison's dead. Pathetic drooling idiots like George Bush Jr. and Ariel Sharon are in charge of important nations (I wouldn't even want to put those guys in charge of a public washroom). We got "dirty bombs" and "smart bombs" and crazy high school kids with guns. If there's no Heaven and no bright future somewhere down the road, why shouldn't we just hang our heads and moan? If we can't believe that this ugly old world isn't just one manifestation of the Infinite Spectrum of Mind how can we possibly be expected to carry on? The best we can muster is stoic perseverance in the face of endless despair. How can anyone say that a philosophy which insists this world is all there is be called bright and optimistic?

Because the problems you have are in your mind. Yeah, you read right. Pollution, WWIII, dead Beatles, rotten Presidents, bombs and all that other stuff is all in your head. Am I saying those problems don't exist? No. Am I saying that stuff isn't a problem, that these things don't need to be addressed and corrected? Certainly not. What I am saying is that all that stuff is in the realm of thought and in the realm of thought nothing is ever right. There is no Heaven because even if you went to Heaven you'd complain about all the harp music.

See, there's reality and then there's our problems. Two different things entirely. If you want to do something about pollution, WWIII, rotten Presidents and the rest, by all means do it. Just don't make a problem out of it. That's where we go wrong.

The reason Buddhists reject ideas about Heaven isn't because we think that this vast Universe could not possibly include a place where people with wings wear robes and fly around playing little harps. Maybe it does. Heck, maybe we even go there when we die (I'd rather go to Hawaii). Maybe there's an Infinite Spectrum of Mind in which all these places exist. Maybe you'll get rich and famous someday and all your dreams will come true. How the Hell should I know? The point is that it does not matter. What matters is where and what you are right here and right now. "The kingdom of Heaven is within you," the Bible says. So is the Infinite Spectrum of Mind. It's right there with Godzilla, UFOs, that trip you took to Florida back in 1972 with Neil Diamond playing on the radio and all the rest.

This doesn't mean you can't have any fun. In fact, it means quite the opposite. We don't need to believe in strange fantasies to have fun. Life is much better without them. Godzilla isn't real, but Godzilla movies are. The same applies to whatever you might enjoy in life. The Infinite Spectrum of Mind is a lovely idea. Enjoy it as such, if you like. Just don't make a problem out of it by insisting that it has to be real, by insisting that your ideas about reality are reality itself. Don't replace reality with your own beliefs.

The beliefs we have should be reasonable. The way Buddhist use the word reason is a little different from the common understanding of the word. Reason involves intuition, not merely thought. True intuition is not some kind of vague feeling. It is crystal clear, much clearer than thought or sensory perception. Yet putting such intuition into words is difficult and will always be inexact. It isn't so hard to understand why this is so. You can pick up a flower, hold it in your hands, look at it color and smell its fragrance. But try putting that into words. Yet for some strange reason we tend to think that putting a philosophy about the whole Universe into words should be easier.

Reality is here and now. The Universe is where you are at this moment. The most important action you can possibly take is what you do right now. Be completely naked. Be absolutely open and the Universe will show itself in all of its true colors. God will stand before you and within you.

AFTERWORD

I don't remember who Mr. Spectrum was. But I remember talking about this incident to one of the people who used to come to Nishijima's talks regularly but who wasn't at this one. He knew exactly who I was talking about. Mr. Spectrum didn't come to all of Nishijima's talks. But he was a frequent enough visitor that he was known to the regular group. I wish I could tell you what became of him, but I have no idea.

It could be argued that there is some precedent in Dogen's philosophy for the idea of the Infinite Spectrum of Mind. In his Shobogenzo essay called *Inmo* (variously translated as "Suchness" or "It") Dogen says, "The universe in ten directions is just one small part of the supreme truth of Bodhi." One could read this as indicating that the entire universe we live in is just one small slice of something much bigger and more vast. I don't think that would be a mistaken understanding.

But on that day, at that lecture, that guy Mr. Spectrum wasn't really saying this, even if he thought he was. What he was saying was more like, "Acknowledge me! Acknowledge my fantasies about something like Heaven that I'm too clever to call Heaven anymore!" To him, the Infinite Spectrum of Mind was the Great Beyond, a paradise in the sky that one could focus on while ignoring the day-to-day realities of real existence. It was this that Nishijima Roshi was denying.

There are a lot of examples in Buddhism of a student seemingly expressing exactly what his teacher has taught him only to be told by the teacher that this is absolutely wrong. The most famous of these stories is the one about Gutei's finger. Zen Master Gutei always taught by holding up one finger. When he found out his disciple was imitating him by also holding up one finger, the master called him into his room and chopped off the disciple's finger. This probably didn't literally happen. I doubt that any Zen Master would ever cut off someone's finger just to make a point. Maybe he grabbed the disciple's finger and twisted it or something like that, and like any good "fish story" the incident got exaggerated in the re-telling. The point is that the disciple was just aping the superficial aspects of his teacher's teachings without understanding their spirit.

I'm not sure that was really the case with Mr. Spectrum. I think he just wanted to have his interpretation of things approved by the master. Nishijima Roshi was the wrong guy to turn to if you wanted that.

There's No Future for You

CHAPTER 14

THE TEN THOUSAND THINGS

INTRODUCTION

I don't think I wrote this article very well. It comes off as defensive. In some ways maybe it is defensive. But I was intending to convey something more universal. It's not just about me. At least it's not supposed to be. I was hoping to communicate what I had learned from Nishijima Roshi about how to be myself completely.

The catalyst for writing this was my being accused of being arrogant. I thought about that and remembered how I thought Nishijima Roshi was insufferably arrogant when I first encountered him. It took a while for me to understand that what I interpreted as arrogance really wasn't anything of the kind. Nishijima was fully and unapologetically himself. There's a big difference.

On the other hand, there is value in being able to speak and behave in ways that polite society perceives not to be arrogant. I'm working on that.

THE ARTICLE

Isn't life fun? Just the other day a weird little e-mail came to me from someone who'd seen this silly little Zen website.

The mail went something like this: "Nobody who knows anything of Zen Buddhism in today's Japan would presume automatically that because one has been transmitted that one is as a matter of consequence a master of Zen. Your oblique tooting of your own horn is so typically crass of the American immaturity when it comes to Zen and Buddhist practice."

Nice fellow, huh? But he was right. These days in Japan, Dharma Transmission is often given for a variety of reasons, most of which have nothing at all to do with the recipient's understanding of Buddhism. In a great many cases it's simple nepotism, if dad runs a temple, his eldest son is expected to take over when he retires. Sometimes the reasons are political. But even this is nothing new. Dogen wrote about his disgust with similar practices he saw in China 800 years ago. At any rate, the writer's point is well taken. Dharma Transmission is new enough in the West that there aren't quite so many transmissions done solely for reasons like these in America and Europe as there are in Japan. Still, this alone is no basis by which to make any judgements.

My e-mail buddy's other point was valid as well. I do come off as obnoxious and arrogant. I am. Terribly, terribly arrogant. There's no way around it. The only difference between my kind of arrogance and the common variety is that I don't really take it seriously. I'm arrogant about what I am. But I know that what I am is pretty much nothing. I'm one of those little tiny dogs that barks real loud. I am arrogant because I am the best Brad Warner there'll ever be and I have no problems with that*. And what's more, I think the world would be a better place with more of this kind of arrogance.

So I wrote the guy back saying he was absolutely right and asking where he was from. I always like to know where people who are writing me are from. It's neat getting e-mail from exotic places. Since he'd made a point of calling my arrogance typically American and since he'd titled his mail "Utter Arse" I figured he had to be from some other English speaking country, maybe Britain, or Ireland. Do they say "arse" for "ass" in Australia? I don't know. And how can something be "utter ass" anyway? Whatever.

So this is what I get back: "You asked where I am from. I ask you about the Ten Thousand Things, we are told they return to the One, to whence does the One return? To say it never left home is the Truth but does not hit the mark. How shall you answer?"

Jesus, dude, what are you smoking over there (wherever you are)? This kind of thing is one of the hazards of the job, I guess—"Buddhist" guys who want to play Dharma combat with you via e-mail.

Dharma combat is a dubious practice to begin with. Dharma combat, for those of you who have better things to do than waste your time reading books about arcane old Buddhist practices, is where Buddhist monks ask each other ridiculous unanswerable questions. Whoever stays sane longest wins. I'd made the mistake of asking where the guy was from, which is a typical kind of question you find in old accounts of famous Dharma combats. These accounts and the questions within them are known as "koans" which literally means "public case." My buddy's ten thousand things story is one, so is the old favorite; What is the sound of one hand clapping? But only a real doofus would think you can do that by e-mail. The whole thing with Dharma combat is that it's not really so much what your opponent answers as how he or she answers, how much hesitation, what tone of voice, the posture. It's not a competition, but a way of deepening both participants' understanding of Buddhism. None of that comes across in an e-mail. And anyway, as I said before, it's not something I put a whole lot of stock in to begin with. Yet if you log on to any Buddhist chat group you'll find at least half a dozen Zen dudes engaged in the amazingly constructive practice of idiotic fake

Dharma combat. Some guys love this even more than Tetris.

I have to check out the monster movie chat groups as part of my job and I see the exact same thing there. People will bitch and moan at each other over the proper romanization of the name of the chief cameraman on *War of the Gargantuas*. I've actually seen people get really vicious over garbage like this! Wherever nerds gather you'll find this kind of behavior. Zen nerds do precisely the samething, all trying to prove to everyone else that they're the biggest nerd of all. Zen guys should be smart enough to know it doesn't matter.

Unfortunately, reality isn't always what you expect it to be.

The answer I gave my e-mail friend, by the way, was that I grew up near Akron, Ohio. Let him try and find deep meaning in that! I got your ten thousand things. Right here...

*Apologies to other people named Brad Warner, but you know what I'm getting at.

AFTERWORD

My e-mail buddy eventually told me he was from London. But the exchange petered out fast when he realized I had no interest in engaging in the debate he'd set up. This wasn't the first time someone had tried to engage me in dharma combat via email and it would not be the last. Lots of people have lots of strange ideas about engaging in discussions about Buddhist matters. The Internets are full of people throwing clichés they've read in Buddhist books at each other. I'm just not interested.

The specific cliché my email buddy brings up about the ten-thousand things returning to the one is not one of my favorites. It's very intellectual. And in being so intellectual it's actually pretty easy. My answer most days would probably be something like, "Blehhhhh!" or "Your mom is Ten Thousand Things!" In other words, the koan sets up a problem that can't possibly be solved intellectually. So the proper response is to refuse to be drawn into the categories the question sets up for you. Of course if you know that and respond based on your knowledge, you'll still fail the test because you'll be responding again from the intellect.

I'm not sure what this guy expected or intended by asking me that stuff via email. I can't envision any response that would have satisfied him. So I didn't try. I figure the best way to deal with someone like this is to try and engage them in normal human conversation. But that didn't work either because he just wanted to argue with someone.

As for arrogance, I still think a kind of conscious arrogance can be a very good thing. I grew up believing that I should apologize for what I was. I was never "normal." I'm not sure anyone is ever truly "normal." But some people value normality and are very good at convincing others that they have achieved that rarified state. I never could, even when I tried. I remember once trying an experiment with a girlfriend. We decided we would be "normal" for a whole day. We would say normal things to each other and to anyone we met and we'd behave in normal ways. This broke down in about half an hour.

Little children don't worry a lot about being normal. They're fully themselves. But we all lose that as we grow older. Nishijima Roshi sometimes used to say that the point of zazen practice was "to come back to our childhood." It's to learn the kind of arrogance children have before they learn to care what other people think of them. We'd all be happier if we cared less what other people think of us.

CHAPTER 15

ZEN AND THE ART OF WRITING

INTRODUCTION

At last! Something useful. I can't remember where the writing workshop I wrote this for was. I don't even recall leading any writing workshops ever, at least not early in my career. But I guess I must have.

I think this stuff is still good advice, and it's still what I do. It was kind of funny reading this again so many years later. I remember about a year ago I was trying to start a band with a friend of mine. I told her that I wanted to avoid any hint of "self expression." At the time I thought this was something I'd only just started getting into. But it seems like I've had that idea for a long time.

THE ARTICLE

I was asked to host a workshop about writing this weekend. Here's the text I prepared for the workshop.

I can't recall a time when I didn't enjoy writing. As a child I made my own comic books, graduating later to short science fiction stories and comical poems (I thought I saw a pig, but he was doing a jig, I know that this sounds dumb, but he was on my thumb...). Though I'm not what most people think of as a professional writer, my job as the overseas publicity guy for Tsuburaya

Productions (makers of Ultraman) involves a lot of writing. I write all of the company's overseas promotional material, including fliers, press releases, and promotional videos. I even wrote an episode of the *Ultraman Gaia* TV series. Unfortunately, that particular episode was axed at the last minute by the network who were concerned about its premise (my episode took place in an alternate universe where Ultraman was the bad guy and the monsters were the good guys). A few of my short stories have made it into print and I've also written three novels which remain unpublished.

My involvement with Zen Buddhism began in 1983 when I was a student at Kent State University (KSU) in Kent, Ohio. I'd been interested in Eastern religions since I was 10. My family lived in Nairobi, Kenya then, where my dad worked for the Firestone Tire Company. One of my dad's best friends was an Indian man named Ramesh Wanza. Whenever we visited Ramesh's house I was fascinated by the pictures and statues of the Hindu gods. I was also intrigued by the fact that Ramesh's wife and children ate no meat. Years later, when I saw a class called Zen Buddhism being offered by KSU's Experimental College, I signed up. The teacher was Tim McCarthy. His teacher had been Kobun Chino, a Zen priest brought to the US by Shunryu Suzuki. Shunryu Suzuki (not to be confused with D.T. Suzuki) was the author of a very influential book called Zen Mind, Beginner's Mind. I studied with Tim for several years and lived in a small Zendo he set up.

When I moved to Tokyo in 1994, I found a teacher here named Gudo Wafu Nishijima, the author of numerous books about Buddhism including several in English. I've studied and practiced with Nishijima ever since then.

Talking about Zen and the art of writing might seem like a contradiction in terms. One of the main ideas of Zen is that the truth cannot be expressed in words. Verbal or written expressions are compared to a finger pointing at the moon. When someone points out the moon to you, you're supposed to look in the sky, not at his finger. Unless you're a cat. If you try to point something out to a cat they always look at your finger.

It's not just that the so-called Ultimate Truth can't be expressed in words. No truth can be fully expressed in words. Even a phrase like, "I have to go to the toilet," doesn't express the whole truth of the situation. I don't know if you have to go "number one" or "number two," if it's really urgent or if you're just looking for an excuse to get away from this boring lecture, or what.

Still, if you can't see something, it's useful to have someone point it out. So Buddhist teachers write. One of the reasons Buddhism has lasted so long is because of the efforts of centuries of Buddhist writers. Buddhist teachers write in order to teach themselves as much as to teach others. So Zen Buddhism does have something to say to writers. Here are a few things I've learned about writing through my study of Buddhism.

1) YOU DON'T EAT IN ORDER TO TAKE A SHIT

The quote above is a saying by Kodo Sawaki, Gudo Nishijima's Zen teacher. A more polite, though less memorable, way of putting it is, "Don't be concerned with results." Don't worry about whether what you write will or won't sell. Just write. Write for yourself alone. For about two years I had an agent working on selling one of my novels. She couldn't sell the thing, but the editors at three of the publishers she sent it to replied that they personally really liked it. They just didn't think it would sell. And my sister's husband loved it.

I love it too. I can pick it up and read a chapter and feel that it's one of the best books I've ever come across. No one can write the book you most want to read better than you can yourself. So a grand total of six people really enjoyed my book. I'm very pleased with that. If you'd told me before I started writing that only six people would read that novel, I might never have written it. And I would have missed out on something really wonderful.

Maybe you don't even want to write professionally. That's great. This advice can be applied to any kind of writing including e-mails, letters home and even business proposals. Yes, even when you're writing a business proposal, you shouldn't be concerned about results. Write the best, strongest, clearest business proposal you possibly can. But at the moment of writing, focus only on writing and don't give any concern to whether the proposal will succeed or not. Aim for your target. But know that there are a billion other factors involved in whether you hit or miss, and most of these are completely beyond your control. Taking aim is what really matters.

The very concept of success and failure is questionable. What seems like failure can often turn out to be just a different kind of success. Sometimes you succeed masterfully in missing your target. Sometimes missing your goal is exactly what is needed. The idea of a result is just an illusion. Results only appear when we think about time as linear, moving from past through present and into the future. Real time is only this very moment. Right now, what is is what is. No results. No causes.

2) AVOID SELF EXPRESSION

Too many people think writing is about expressing themselves. It's not. What we call our "self" is just an image selected from those parts of the universal human nature we choose to emphasize in our lives. It's not what we really are. As a writer your duty is not to this illusory self, but to the words on the paper, to the story you're telling.

Writers of fiction know that there are times when the characters
they create act in ways they do not expect. The first time this
happened to me was a shock. I'd heard about such things, but
didn't really believe it. After all, it was me, my "self," making up
the story. How could my made-up characters start acting of their
own accord? When they started to, I was amazed. All I could do
was transcribe what they were doing as clearly as possible. I could
no longer manipulate events.

Your personality will come through in your writing. You can't
help it. The point is to let that happen as it happens. Don't try to
demonstrate your personality.

*3) DON'T SAY THINGS UNLESS YOU KNOW WHAT THEY
MEAN*

A few years ago, our Talent Division was managing a 10 year old
half Japanese, half American singer named Nadia. Nadia had
been to America and recorded a duet with Peabo Bryson. The
recording was given a quick mix down in the US, then the master
tapes were shipped to Japan where a Japanese producer remixed
them in a way he thought more suitable for the Japanese market.
Nadia's father, the American half of her parentage, hated the new
mix and wrote a very strong letter to our company. My 73 year
old boss who'd learned English from soldiers during the US Oc-
cupation was asked to translate that into Japanese.

The letter was full of weird idioms and loads of "self expression."
It said nothing about what the real problem with the new mix
was, but did tell us a lot about Nadia's dad's personality. One
expression that stands out in my mind was the phrase, "The
American mix was a TRIBUTE (he wrote the word all in capitals)
to Peabo Bryson's talent." My boss asked me what that phrase
meant. What the heck does that mean? I thought a lot about it,
but couldn't tell him anything more than that Nadia's father liked

the American version better. Phrases like this don't tell the reader anything. They express emotion and outrage in a very vague way. But if this is what you intend to do, "I'm really pissed off," gets to the matter much more directly.

When I write our company's publicity material, I know that most of the readers will be Asian people for whom English is a second language. I have to remember that they read English the way I read Japanese, automatically translating it in their minds as they read. It's a good discipline to have to write for that kind of audience. It forces you to say just what you mean as clearly as possible. Try writing that way sometime.

The last two points don't have so much to do with Zen. But they're useful.

4) DON'T USE TOO MUCH EXPOSITION

When you submit stories to magazines sometimes you get a critique back from the editor. It's usually a printed form with check boxes on it. It's rare to get any kind of personal commentary. But a magazine editor isn't a writing teacher, and he or she has no obligation to even do this much. Whenever I got these, the one box that was always checked off was, "Too much exposition." This is supposed to mean you've given too much description and background information and not enough action. It's good advice. But I followed it to the point where I had absolutely no exposition at all. You didn't know who the characters were, where they were, why they were there, nothing. And still I got the "Too much exposition" box checked off on those little cards. This must be the box you check when you don't really know why you don't like the story.

But beginning writers do generally give the reader too much information. Think about what you notice when you meet a person.

When I see the girls in Shibuya (a district in Tokyo known as a hangout for fashionable young women), I notice they're wearing short skirts and long vinyl boots. Later on if you ask me what else they were wearing and I might answer, "Um, clothes?" Just mention what's important. If you're describing a girl in Shibuya, just mention the skirt and boots. When they make your book into a movie, the producers can worry about the rest of the outfit.

5) EDIT RUTHLESSLY

Write long and then cut out what you don't need. Your first draft is just to get your thoughts down on paper. In your second draft, you add details. In your third draft you take out all the details you really didn't need. Don't worry how long it took you to come up with that gorgeous description of the dew drops lazily rolling down the waxy surface of the holly leaves as the morning sun crept like a swollen blowfish over the flabby brown hills. If it doesn't fit the story, chop it out.

Enjoy what you do and do what you enjoy. When you write, write with all of your being. When you do the dishes, do it like it's the most important thing you've ever done in your life.

Then forget about it.

AFTERWORD

That stuff about describing the girls in Shibuya was inspired by one of my early attempts at short story writing. I was trying to describe a girl and ended up with a long paragraph cataloguing everything she was wearing. That's not a good way to write.

I'm pretty much self-taught when it comes to writing. I learned by looking at books I liked and analyzing them. I remember taking apart short stories by Philip K. Dick and seeing how he

constructed them. I looked at how much description he used
for characters, where he introduced certain information relating
to the plot, the structure of each piece and so on. Sometimes I
wrote my own stories slavishly following the stylistic information
I gathered this way. Sometimes the stories were good, but often
they weren't. It was good practice either way.

There's one big influence on my writing that I don't mention here
because at the time I probably wasn't very aware of it. When I
wrote this piece, one of my main jobs was writing in English for
people whose native language was not English. These were generally TV and film industry people from Asia who communicated
in English with other industry people in different countries. I
had to learn to keep my sentences short and to avoid idiomatic
expressions that didn't translate well.

The guy who said that song's mix was a "TRIBUTE to Peabo
Bryson's talent" was a perfect example of someone communicat-
ing in English in a way that someone who wasn't a native speaker
couldn't possibly understand. My 73 year old boss who asked
about that had been speaking English for perhaps 50 or more
years. In other words, he'd been speaking my language longer
than I'd been alive, and he spoke it extremely well. But because
he wasn't a native speaker expressions like that made no sense to
him. He tried to interpret them literally. I remember him sitting
there with a dictionary looking up all the possible meanings of
the word "tribute" and finding none that corresponded to how it
was used in the letter from Nadia's enraged dad.

As native speakers we all carry around a ton of expressions similar to these that convey certain emotions to other native speakers,
yet when analyzed linguistically make no sense al all. If you learn
to identify and replace those with phrases that make more literal
sense, you'll find you have a better chance of being understood
by a greater number of people. Even some native speakers won't

understand your particular idioms if they happen to be regional. Sometimes it's good to use these kinds of expressions. For example, a novelist who wants to hake a character sound a certain way can use them. I remember a Kurt Vonnegut novel where he makes a point of having a character say, "I like the cut of your jib." This is another one of those nonsense phrases. Vonnegut wanted to establish that the character talked in a certain way. In non-fiction writing, it's usually best to avoid those kinds of expressions.

It's also good to keep your sentences short. When I tried to read Japanese, I noticed that the longer the sentence, the more difficult it was to understand. You can get lost in a long sentence. Try to keep things short. Split long sentences up into briefer ones.

Also, remember that each character should have one name. This goes for fiction and non-fiction. If you introduce about someone named John Stuart Smythe, pick one of those names to refer to him by the next time you mention him. Don't call him John sometimes and Smythe sometimes and JSS sometimes just to mix things up. All you'll mix up will be your readers who will wonder if they're reading about the same guy. I've seen professional writers make this mistake and it's annoying.

In spite of the title of the piece, I feel I don't talk much about the Zen aspect of writing here. There's a little bit of that right at the beginning. But I kind of lose the thread by the end.

For me, the main connection between Zen and writing is that I generally do my writing right after practicing zazen each morning. So I come to the page with a so-called "Zen mind." That doesn't necessarily mean I have cleared my mind. Sometimes the mind in zazen is clear. Sometimes it's not. But in either case, it's had a chance to settle, even if that settling process has been incomplete.

I also practice writing much like I practice zazen. That is to say, I do it over and over and over. I write every day. And most of what I write never gets seen by anyone. Yet this unseen writing is not wasted. It's part of my practice. If a bassist practices the riff from Rapper's Delight by the Sugarhill Gang three hundred times at home, but only once on stage, it doesn't mean that the three hundred times she played it to nobody at all were wasted. Besides, I often find I can use pieces of writing that I did only for practice without any intention of making them public.

A lot of Zen people are artists in various fields. Dogen was a writer or prose and poetry and he left a great legacy. But it's a mistake to think that prose explanations of Zen are somehow superior to explanations of Zen in poetry, painting, calligraphy or other more abstract forms. Often prose expressions can convey very little. We're just used to that form. Sometimes prose appears to be explaining more than it really does. Often it's just intellectual speculation masquerading as explanation.

The Zen approach to writing doesn't mean you arrive at every writing session with a blank mind. It's OK to have an agenda. But you also allow the moment to guide you without forcing your agenda upon it. I often come up with things spontaneously in writing that are far better than what I'd intended to write.

Good luck with your own Zen writing.

Zen And The Art of Writing

CHAPTER 16

THE WHOLE VEGETARIAN THING

INTRODUCTION

I'm a vegetarian. I get asked about the connection between vegetarianism and Buddhism all the time. I think it's a valid question especially since there's a common misapprehension that all Buddhists are vegetarians. They aren't.

The most puzzling thing to me about the piece below is that it was rejected for inclusion in the book *Hardcore Zen*. I believe a version of this appeared on my website, though I'm not entirely certain. I can't find that version, so maybe I imagined it. In any case, the version reproduced here is the one that was included in the first manuscript I submitted to Wisdom Publications for the book that became *Hardcore Zen*. Josh Bartok, my editor, decided that it should be cut. He said something about it not fitting with the flow of the rest of the book. But he was wrong. It fits in perfectly with the rest of the book.

I'm left scratching my head as to why this chapter never made it into the book. But here is what I wrote about being a vegetarian back in 2003.

THE ARTICLE

Another of the beliefs a lot of people have about Buddhist beliefs is that Buddhists are all vegetarians. I'm a vegetarian. When people ask me why, I have two responses I like to use. One comes from a comedian I saw at the Tokyo British Club. "When people ask me why I'm a vegetarian," he said, "I tell them I'm a vegetarian because I don't eat meat. When they ask me when I became a vegetarian, I say I became a vegetarian when I stopped eating meat." The other reply I like is one I made up myself: A lot of people become vegetarians because they love animals, I became a vegetarian because I hate plants.

I've been a vegetarian for nearly 20 years now, so I've heard the question more times than I can count. Most people who ask have no real interest in the answer. They just want a quick reply so they can get onto the next topic. And for some reason there are a whole lot of people who assume that vegetarians enjoy arguing about their dietary preferences. You can tell these folks right away by the tone in which they ask the question. They want you to give a big confrontational answer so they can start a debate, or better yet an all out war of words on the subject. I'm not interested in such debates.

In Japan, I can just tell people I'm a vegetarian because I'm a Buddhist and that usually shuts them up. Most Japanese people don't know that plenty of Japanese Buddhists are not vegetarians. The average Japanese person knows far less about Buddhism than the average Western person who has a passing interest in Eastern philosophy—the kind of person who might buy a book like this one. They've visited temples and seen a few bad documentaries on TV about monks who stand naked under waterfalls. When it comes to Buddhism, Japanese people are easy to fool.

Ever since I first found out what meat really was I was squeamish about eating it. I recall the horror of first learning that sausage casings were made of pig and cow intestines and of noticing ingredients like "beef lips" on my Slim Jim packages. People don't like to tell their kids that bologna is dead cows and pork chops are dead piggies. Like finding out Santa Claus isn't real, it's something you have to learn from the streets.

When I lived in Kenya as a child I was exposed to a lot of Indian vegetarians. You could get samosas-fried spicy Indian pasties filled with potatoes, peas and cauliflower-at any good newsstand. God I loved those things, and still do. I became fascinated with why so many Indians refused to eat meat. Why were cows sacred? When I moved back to Wadsworth, Ohio after three years in Nairobi I found that Scott Wynkoop, my best friend from second grade, along with his mother had become vegetarians. Before I moved to Africa, Scott and I used to love to scarf packages of Slim Jims together. What happened?

Throughout high school I tried unsuccessfully to convert. But it was too much to ask my mom to cook me only veggie food and I sure didn't want to cook for myself! So for a while I made it my practice to eat whatever my mom cooked for me, but to be a vegetarian when I was out by myself. It's a surprisingly Buddhist solution to the problem for someone who'd yet to encounter Buddhism. Buddha told his vegetarian followers they should accept whatever food was put in their begging bowls including meat.

When I got to college, it took me a few month to completely switch over. It was tough to get good vegetarian food with the dorm meal tickets they gave us so I still ate meat sometimes. I remember buying a can of Spam with those tickets. I took it up to my room and ended up cutting my finger while opening the can. My blood dripped onto the meat inside. The symbolism was too clear to ignore. I ate it all somehow, but it wasn't easy. I finally became a convert at Burger King.

Some friends and I had smoked a whole bunch of pot and got a major case of the munchies. We were in no condition to drive and the nearest restaurant was a Burger King. We hoofed it over there, laughing like idiots the whole way. When we got inside it was one of those paranoid situations where you suddenly realize there are straight people around. I composed myself, badly I'm sure, and ordered a Whopper. When I sat down to eat it I became aware of my heartbeat. We'd walked several blocks and my heart was beating faster than usual, not to mention that marijuana can make you more aware of things like that. As I bit into the Whopper, the thought occurred to me that I was eating something which had probably had the same experience as I was having of noticing its own heartbeat. I thought of those red "juices" the commercials always tell you about. What was that stuff really? The answer was too clear. That was it or me. The next day I gave up eating meat.

My decision to stop eating meat was an intuitive matter. I never had a big list of intellectual reasons for it. It's always been difficult for me to come up with good solid fact-based intellectual reasons for not eating meat. None of many the reasons people keep giving me as to why I should start eating meat again have been convincing either. The fact, pointed out to me by a surprising number of people, that Jesus Christ ate lamb and fish never held much weight for me. Nor have I felt particularly unhealthy since giving up meat.

Phillip Kapleau wrote a book called *To Cherish All Life: A Buddhist View of Animal Slaughter and Meat Eating* which gives a lot of good reasons based on Buddhist philosophy to be a vegetarian. Frances Moore Lappé's *Diet for a Small Planet* is another good one, I've heard. I've never actually read it. And, of course, the Hare Krishnas can give you a thousand good reasons to give up eating meat if you want that sort of thing. All of the reasons these books give are good. The fact that the human digestive system is not constructed like those of meat eating animals and has tremendous difficulty even processing the stuff, is especially convincing. But my own reasons were never so intellectually sound. To put it simply, I don't eat meat because I do not like eating meat. Meat doesn't even seem like food to me anymore. I no more crave to eat a slice of fried cow leg than the average meat eater craves to eat a dead cat or a handful of wriggling worms. To my way of thinking these days, meat simply doesn't come under the category of "Things to Eat" anymore than dirt or rocks or wet cardboard would.

One argument I've heard a few hundred times to justify meat eating is that even vegetarians have to kill things to eat. This is true. And it is a very important point for vegetarians to bear in mind. We may not be slaughtering cows or pigs, but we're killing cabbages, potatoes and carrots. These things are alive too and there is considerable evidence that they have a kind of primitive survival instinct. Plants connected to EEG machines are known to react in measurable ways when they are hurt or even when another plant nearby is attacked.

You cannot live without causing violence. Vegetarians, vegans, fruitarians and even Jain monks-who not only eat nothing but fruit but also sweep away bugs from their paths with little whisk brooms as they walk-cannot completely avoid causing harm to others while they live. The very act of living itself is a kind of violence.

But I'm quick to point out to people who use this argument, that there are different levels of violence. It's a criminal act to kill a human being, but it's not a crime to kill a cow. So we acknowledge there is a difference. If there's a difference between killing a man and killing a cow, then there is also a difference between killing a cow and killing a carrot. Being a vegetarian is not without violence, but it is a considerably less violent way of life than that of eating meat.

Eating meat makes a person feel more aggressive. It certainly does that to me on the rare occasions when I do eat a bit of the stuff these days. The reason is simple. When an animal is slaughtered it inevitably feels threatened. I've watched chickens being killed in Kenya and they are not any more willing to give up their lives for Colonel Sanders than you would be. These animals tense up and release a lot of adrenaline and other chemicals into their bloodstreams when it dawns on them what's about to happen. This highly agitated state is passed on to the person who eats the meat. Certainly there are aggressive vegetarians. Meat eating isn't the only thing that makes people violent. But it heightens the aggressive tendencies we already have and we really don't need that.

Gautama Buddha was a staunch opponent to the practice of animal sacrifice. In fact, when Buddhism began to die off in India to be replaced by a resurgence of Brahmanism (what's commonly called Hinduism today), Buddha was incorporated into the Brahmanistic pantheon as a minor incarnation of the god Vishnu. Vishnu appeared on Earth as Buddha, the latter day Brahmanists teach, to halt the practice of animal sacrifice.

There's a story that someone who owned a pet dog once came to Buddha. Buddha told the dog's owner that the dog didn't trust him completely because he ate meat. The dog, Buddha said, could smell the odor of meat from his owner's body and was therefore always secretly afraid his owner would one day eat him. If he wanted the dog to truly love him, Buddha said, he should give up eating meat.

When Buddhism reached China, the practice of monks begging for food was no longer practical. Indian culture supported begging monks, but the Chinese had no such tradition. Vegetarianism became the norm in Chinese monasteries as it had become in the Indian Buddhist monasteries. In fact, tofu is said to have been invented by Chinese Buddhist monks looking for a substitute for meat in their diet. So tofu haters around the world can blame the Buddhists. Buddhist monasteries in Japan followed suit.

Eating meat is not regarded as something sinful by Buddhists as it is by many Brahmanists and by certain Christian and Jewish sects who do not eat meat. Buddha told his followers that if an animal was not slaughtered specifically for them to eat, there was no bad karmic influence from eating its meat. I think I speak for most vegetarians, though, when I say that we tend to feel terribly guilty if we end up having to eat meat for some reason. I know I do. But feeling guilty isn't so useful.

The guilt we veggies feel at these times is too idealistic. We view ourselves as people who do not eat meat, and eating meat spoils that self image. A lot of Zen teachers are known to try and trick their militant vegetarian students into eating meat. They'll force you into some weird social situation where it's nearly impossible to refuse to eat what you're given, then suddenly present you with a big, juicy steak or something. There's a story about Shunryu Suzuki once going to a roadside burger stand and ordering a hamburger for himself while a strict vegetarian student of his ordered a grilled cheese. When the order came, Suzuki grabbed the grilled cheese, popped it in his mouth, then handed his student the burger and said, "Here, you eat mine."

When I first went to one of Nishijima's Zen retreats, I expected that the temple food would be strictly vegetarian as it usually is in Japanese temples. So I was pretty surprised on the final day when I saw pieces of ground beef in the mixed vegetable dish we were served. Meals at Zen temples are served in a very formal way. You are expected to eat everything you're served and there's no talking. I was trapped. In those days I was still a pretty tight assed vegetarian and it was hard to choke that stuff down. But I did it. I felt horrible afterwards.

Maybe this was a lesson of some sort, I thought. When I asked Nishijima about it he answered, "How do you know that cow felt pain?" The answer got me so steamed, I couldn't reply. Years later I asked him about that incident and he just said, "I'm very sorry if my thoughtless answer bothered you." Damn Zen Masters...

I always wondered why my teachers were able to eat meat. I actually started to feel a little bad about being a vegetarian, like maybe a true Buddhist should have no attachments at all, even to not eating meat. I've had conversations with both Tim and Nishijima about this. And though both of them did eat meat (Tim only ate chicken on the advice of his doctor because he was allergic to so many vegetables), both of them advised me to continue being a vegetarian. I can recall thinking that no matter how enlightened I ever got, I couldn't get to the point where eating meat seemed like an acceptable thing for me to do. Other people made their own choices. But it wasn't for me.

There are rare occasions now when I will eat meat. Once when my wife's parents stayed with us they bought themselves some take-away chicken curry. They didn't finish it so we decided to eat the left-overs rather than throw them away. It seemed more right to eat the chicken than to waste it. I discovered two things about eating chicken for the first time in two decades. One was that it tasted good. I won't deny that. But the surprising thing was that, though I liked the taste, I did not enjoy eating it. I didn't feel guilty about it or that I was going to incur bad karma or suddenly have the urge to beat someone up. I just did not want to eat meat. There are Buddhists I've met who seem to think they're far more enlightened because they eat meat. I was present when one such teacher was asked by a young person just starting to get interested in Buddhism if he was a vegetarian. He proudly declared, "No, I eat steak sometimes." I piped in that I didn't. It's hard for me to generate too much respect for that kind of attitude. Whatever your dietary choices, it's important not to get too proud of them.

It's a true shame to see how lightly most people take the act of eating. I was at a restaurant the other day, a vegetarian place in fact, and the man sitting next to me not only read a magazine while he ate, but had on a pair of headphones and took the occasional glance up at the TV set that blared away in the corner. I kept wondering how he even managed to aim his chopsticks so the food would land in his mouth.

The highly ritualized way in which meals are served at Buddhist monasteries isn't just for show. Those rituals are there to remind us that eating is something we should never take lightly. Eating is a very important activity.

In the formal dining ceremony at Zen temples you have no choice but to pay close attention to the act of eating. You're given a set of three bowls wrapped in a white cloth called oriyoki. When one of the monks sounds a loud bell, everyone rushes to the dining room with their oriyoki set. You stand around the low tables holding your oriyoki at forehead level until the teacher comes in. He or she sits (I'll pretend your teacher's a "he" from here on), then you sit. There are no chairs, you sit on thin cushions on the floor. The teacher bangs a pair of wooden clappers together and you all recite the following together;

Gautama Buddha was born in Kapira

Attaining the truth in Makada,

he preached the teachings in Harana

and died in Kuchira.

Awakened Buddha, I have gotten the utensils for eating.

Now I open them. I pray that all living beings will find the same.

May those who eat meals, those who serve meals,

and the meals themselves be serene and undisturbed

Then a monk comes around with the food. The master gets his first and then the rest are served. One bowl is filled with miso soup, one with pickled daikon radishes, one with rice and, if you're lucky, you'll get a fourth bowl of vegetables. As each serving is doled out it's your job to tell the server through a few established gestures—no talking is allowed—how much you want. You are expected to eat everything you receive, so don't take too much. But you have to remember to save at least one of your slices of pickled radish. Once all the food has been served, the teacher hits those clappers again, you hold your rice bowl up to your forehead and chant the next verse.

We reflect firstly on the insufficiency of our effort in this life.

We contemplate the effort which has gone into the preparation of this meal.

We reflect secondly upon our merit.

We know that we are not deserving of this meal.

We reflect thirdly upon the sources of our mental illusions and mistakes.

We must avoid greed, anger and ignorance.

We reflect fourthly upon the reasons for eating meals.

It is to avoid becoming weak and thin.

Finally we reflect upon the ultimate reason for taking meals.

It is only to attain the truth.

Our meal is in three parts.

The upper portion is for the Three Treasures: Buddha, Dharma and Sangha

The middle portion is for the Four Honored Ones: our parents, our rulers, sentient beings and the Universe itself.

The lower portion is for the six kinds of beings, from the gods to the dwellers in hell.

We serve meals to all equally. They are not for us alone.

We eat the upper portion to cut the wrong, the middle portion to promote the good and the last to save all living beings.

May all living beings attain the truth.

After that you can eat. But keep your eye on your teacher. When

he puts down his chopsticks, everybody puts down their chopsticks. The head serving monk yells, "Sai shin!" (seconds). The
servers come around again. Once they're done, you eat some
more. But when your teacher puts his chopsticks on top of his
rice bowl, everybody stops. Tea is served next. They come around
and pour it in your rice bowl, so you'd better not have any more
rice still left over. After the tea, a monk comes around and pours
hot water in your bowl. Use the piece of pickled radish you
saved—you didn't eat the last one, I hope!—to slosh the water
around and knock off any bits of food that might be stick to the
sides of the bowl. Drink a bit of water and pour the rest into the
slightly smaller middle bowl, slosh, drink, and pour the rest into
the smallest bowl. Don't drink the rest. A monk will come around
with a bowl to collect the remaining water. This is traditionally
looked upon as a gift to hungry ghosts who may be wandering
around near the temple. Usually the birds end up eating it instead. Now dry off your bowls with the cloth they were wrapped
in, and wrap them up. When the teacher sees everyone is done,
he claps the clappers again, and a final verse is chanted

> *This water which has been used to wash our O-Ryoki*
>
> *Has a taste like the sweet rain of heaven.*
>
> *We offer it to countless gods and demons alike.*
>
> *May it serve all living beings and bring them perfect con-
> tentment.*

Everyone rises, bows, the teacher leaves and then you can go.

Traditionally Zen temples had just two meals a day, breakfast and
lunch. But these days dinner is served as well in most places. The

meals don't vary much. The bowl of veggies changes, but the rest stays the same. Japanese people tend to have the image that temple food is incredibly bland. Yet there are expensive restaurants all over the country that specialize in shojin ryori, temple food. Maybe bland is good sometimes. At my first weekend retreat with Nishijima, several of the young people from his company commented that they had expected the food to be worse than it was.

Most of us eat in a really thoughtless way. We walk along the street stuffing french fries in our faces or slouch in front of the TV shoveling Cheetoes into our mouths. We never appreciate what it is we're doing. And the few times we do appreciate it, we're fussy. We don't want to eat that stuff. Our steak isn't cooked well enough. There's too little spice. We can't eat at McDonald's, there's got to be a Burger King around here somewhere. Once you've had that flame broiled taste you'll never go back to fried burgers!

You should look at your food. It's part of you. Literally. That stuff you eat is what's going to make up your body and mind. It is going to be transformed into you; your body and your thoughts, your personality, your being. You don't believe your thoughts are influenced by the chemicals in those Hostess Ding Dongs? Your Cheetoes are your future. Don't neglect them. Look at your food. Taste it. Chew it well and swallow. If it tastes good enjoy the flavor. If it tastes bad enjoy the bad taste. Remember the episode of Star Trek: The Next Generation where Lt. Data, the android character, got fitted with a new computer chip that allowed him to experience human emotions? He could already eat and drink, though apparently, being an android, he really didn't need to. In one scene after he's got his new chip he's in Ten Forward, the Starship Enterprise's lounge. He orders himself a drink, takes a swallow and exclaims with great joy, "I hate this!" Then he takes another big gulp and says, "Yes! I really, really hate this! Give me another!" You have to be just like that.

Appreciate your food. Whether it was a cow or a carrot, something died so that you could enjoy your meal. Something gave up its life for you. Don't ever take that sacrifice lightly. You have a sacred duty to the lives you have claimed. They died so that you could live. Don't let their sacrifice be in vain. Don't fail to appreciate the good they did for you.

A lot of hard work went into getting you that food. Fields were plowed, watered, fertilized, plants and animals were tended to. The produce was loaded onto trucks and hauled vast distances all by people whose hard work went underpaid and unappreciated. Advertising campaigns were launched. Artists were hired for pitiful money to create little characters and designs for the packages. Other guys made up catchy names for the snack food and memorable little jingles so you'd recognize those names when you got to the store. All those people worked very hard for your sake. Literally they worked for you whether they knew it or not. Buddha is said to have been moved to begin his practice when, as a small child, he watched a field being plowed and saw a worm cut in two in the process. In seeing the sacrifices and work that went into providing him with food to eat, he was inspired to action. He knew his life had to be worthy of these tremendous sacrifices being made every day on his behalf.

I wouldn't be a vegetarian unless I thought it was a good thing personally. I'd recommend pretty much anyone to at least try it. There may be times when you need to eat meat, when it would help build up your strength. There's a story about one of Dogen's monks who took ill and requested to be allowed to eat some meat. Dogen agreed. When the other monks questioned Dogen about it, he told them that he watched the monk when he ate meat. He said he saw a demon sitting on the monk's head who snatched away the meat and ate it for himself every time the monk tried to put it in his mouth.

It's a funny story. Dogen wasn't the kind of guy to want to push a literal belief in things like demons. I wonder what he meant.

Whatever you eat, you need to develop a true appreciation for the very act of eating. Plenty of people say that you create your own reality. But Buddhists take this absolutely literally. So all of us have created a world in which we have to eat several times a day. We must really enjoy it then, or we wouldn't have manifested ourselves as creatures that need to do it so often.

What's more important than whether you eat meat or not, is how you eat, how you approach your food, what eating means to you.

AFTERWORD

Dang! That was a lot of words! I don't really think there's that much more to say on the subject. I'm still a vegetarian and I'm still happy with that lifestyle choice.

When I got into Zen, I started hearing all the counter arguments against vegetarianism. And there are a lot of them. The most compelling one I've heard recently is that conscious meat consumption is less environmentally destructive and can be personally healthier than the kind of willy-nilly vegetarianism most of us veggies practice.

To give just one example, a lot of vegetarians refuse to buy leather. I did for a long time. I'd go to places like discount shoe stores to get imitation leather shoes instead. Then I realized I was probably supporting child labor and sweatshops through those purchases. Now I buy leather shoes again.

I'm far too lazy to get as deeply into this kind of stuff as some folks do. But it's just one example of how a decision to be mindful of the suffering of animals can lead you to create more suffering among people.

The problem of vegetarianism in Zen practice is that it so often becomes a huge mental block. Being vegetarian can be a tremendous way of defining the ego. This is why you'll hear stories of Zen teachers tricking their veggie students into eating meat.

As a vegetarian, I do not campaign for people to give up meat. Unless you're really committed to giving up meat, becoming a vegetarian can lead to a lot of cognitive dissonance and general weirdness. Mad craving for meat coupled with a hard attitude of suppressing your desires tends to make a person neurotic and outweighs the general feeling of well-being that many vegetarians get from their dietary choice.

The Whole Vegetarian Thing

CHAPTER 17

WORKING FOR MONSTERS

INTRODUCTION

It's quite possible that a lot of you who purchased this ebook will find this final chapter boring and end up skipping over it. But I don't find it boring at all. And it's also possible that I'm wrong. Maybe you'll like it.

The reason I say that is because the original manuscript of *Hardcore Zen* contained a lot more details about my work at Tsuburaya Productions (more about them in the article below) than the final version. My editor cut these details out because he said we were making a book about Zen and not a book about making monster movies. I wanted to do both, but there ya go. He said that people who bought books about Zen didn't want to hear about cheezy monster movies. I could see the logic in that. So I wasn't overly sad when the details about my monster movie life ended up on the proverbial cutting room floor.

Years later Mike Keller from a magazine called *Monster Attack Team* asked me to write an article about my time working with Tsuburaya. It was easy-peasy to write that article because all I had to do was dig out the original manuscript of *Hardcore Zen* and find all the monster movie related parts that had been cut out. I added a few transitional bits here and there and a couple of more recent observations near the end and *voila*! I had me an article! Now you have it too.

THE ARTICLE

In the 60s and 70s there were plenty of kids out there, who now number among the readers of this magazine, that read Japanese Giants and JFFJ, were members of the Godzilla Fan Club, audio taped every *kaiju* (Japanese giant monster) movie that came on UHF TV (no video tapes yet) and generally geeked out on all things *kaiju*. But how many of those kids went on to grow up and work for one of the leading makers of Japanese fantasy films? As far as I know the answer is one. And that one was me.

Sure Norman England got to know the leading lights of the genre, sat in on the making of every recent Godzilla film and even made his own Japanese sci-fi masterpiece (The Idol). And sure there were others who made lasting friendships with the masters of the craft and contributed greatly to the body of knowledge on the subject. They wrote books, published magazines, and did all sorts of great stuff. But I'm still the only one who ever managed to land himself a full-time job at one of the companies that made our favorite films, and even managed to keep that job for a decade and a half. Which is not to say that what I did was in any way better than what anyone else did. Just that it was unique. And up till now I've never really told the story in print. So here it is.

After years of frustration trying to make my indie-label band Dimentia 13 popular, I moved to Japan in 1993 to work as an English teacher as part of the JET (Japan Exchange and Teaching) program, sponsored by the Japanese Ministry of Education. At the end of my first year in the tiny town of Takaoka, all of my English teacher friends announced they were going back home. I knew I wanted to stay in Japan, but I was tired of the English teaching racket.

I'd been buying *kaiju* related books the entire time I'd been in the country in an attempt not only to build up my collection but to hone my reading skills. I had recently bought a book called "Speaking of Ultraman" (ウルトラマンを語る *Urutoraman wo Kataru*) by Noboru Tsuburaya, son of special effects maestro Eiji Tsuburaya and president of Tsuburaya Productions, the makers of Ultraman. This was the very first book I'd ever bought in Japanese that had no pictures. But I was bound and determined to actually *read* the damned thing rather than just drool over the photos!

In the book Noboru talked extensively about his desire to make Ultraman as popular in America as it was in Japan. A crazy thought occurred to me. I knew that lots of Japanese companies that were interested in what they called "internationalization" liked to hire foreigners to work as liaisons to the West. Maybe Tsuburaya Productions might want to have someone like me on staff to help Noboru realize his dreams. After all, I too shared his desire to see Ultraman succeed in America. In fact, I knew Ultraman could be a big hit in the USA if the right people handled it. And who could be more right than me?

So I wrote him a letter telling him just how great I'd be for his company. I had my girlfriend transform my mutant Japanese into something readable and dashed it off. No answer. About a month later I decided to give it one more shot. So I wrote another letter. The first one had been almost like fan mail with just a hint that I might like to work for the company. The second one was far more direct. I sold myself hard. I put the letter in the mail and decided that was that. If they didn't answer this one, I was just going to stick with my plan to continue the drudgery of the English teaching grind.

Just when I'd almost forgotten the whole thing I came home one night to find a message on my answering machine from the man himself, Mr. Noboru Tsuburaya, asking me to call his secretary to arrange for an interview. I was astounded. I immediately booked a bus ticket for Tokyo. The interview went exceedingly well and a couple weeks later I was offered the job.

Funny thing was, though, the job hadn't really even existed until Noboru decided to hire me. Nobody really had any idea what they were supposed to do with me. For the first several weeks I was told just to go through the files and read everything. I learned a whole lot this way.

I discovered that United Artists had drawn up a contract to purchase the rights to run the *Return of Ultraman* TV series in America as a follow-up to the first Ultraman show, which they were already airing on their loose affiliation of UHF stations. Yet the contract was never signed by the Japanese side. Nobody I spoke to knew precisely why it hadn't been executed since none of them had been at the company at that time. I never did find out. But it was one of many such intriguing dead ends on the road to Ultraman's American success that I discovered in the files.

I was about to become part of one of those dead ends. At the time I was hired, the company was just wrapping up production of a series titled *Ultraman: The Ultimate Hero*, shot entirely on location in Hollywood. From the material in the files I learned that the production had been fraught with frustration, arguments and general dissatisfaction among nearly everyone involved on both sides of the Pacific.

The miniature sets in the first episode had been constructed out of discarded cardboard refrigerator boxes. And it showed! The results were so pathetic a team of Japanese model makers had been sent over to build more suitable buildings. But even the improved miniatures didn't help when the monster costumes created by the American special effects team proved to be too flimsy to hold up during the fights with Ultraman. As a result the hero battled his enemies mainly by shoving them rather gingerly.

The show had none of the adventure or excitement needed to be a success. Every US network that saw the show passed on buying it and it was quietly buried after a brief run on laser disc and VHS in Japan. I ended up ghost writing a fair amount of the correspondence that ended our association with the US production company. Our execs would explain what they wanted to say in Japanese, I'd transcribe that, turn it into a fax in English, dash it off and then wait for their response, which I'd translate into Japanese for our management.

With their first excursion into the US market such a massive disaster the company was naturally shy about jumping into another US/Japanese co-production. It was decided the best thing to do was to put energy into reviving Ultraman in Japan. Tsuburaya Productions had not made an all-new Ultraman TV series in Japan since 1980. So a plan was hatched to revive the character in a series to be titled *Ultraman Neos*.

Everyone in the company was invited to contribute ideas for the show. Inspired by the recent *Star Trek: Voyager* series, I suggested that we make the captain of the science patrol team a woman and invite Hiroko Sakurai, who had played Fuji in the original series to play the role. Naoyuki Eto, head of the company's Planning Department, liked the idea of a female captain but thought Hiroko Sakurai wasn't the person for the part. When the show *Ultraman Tiga* came out in 1996, the commander of the team was a woman. Yep. That was my idea!

I contributed a number of other ideas, most of which were too freaky to be taken very seriously. One of them was an episode in which aliens from another dimension would move Ultraman Neos into our world, a world in which Ultraman Neos was just a character in a TV series and monsters were men in rubber costumes. One scene had the human hero of the show, the one who transforms into Ultraman Neos, mobbed on the streets by little children wanting his autograph. The idea was rejected as too weird. But several years later it was used as the basis for the movie *Ultraman Gaia: The Battle in Hyperspace*. I never received credit or even acknowledgement that I had contributed the basic plot line and some of the key scenes of that film. If the same thing had happened in Hollywood I could have sued for a ton of money!

My job eventually developed into being the guy in the international division who knew about Ultraman. The rest of the international division staff had been hired primarily as business people. They had no interest at all in *kaiju* films. I became the company's professional English speaking fanboy.
But the job wasn't quite as sweet as it might sound. Noboru Tsuburaya became ill with stomach cancer only a few months after I joined the company. He died in 1995, not quite a year after he hired me. Not only was it emotionally devastating, but Noboru's death left me in limbo. It was Noboru who had wanted to make Ultraman successful in America. His son Kazuo, now president and CEO of the company had no such ambitions.

Noboru's far-ranging international marketing dream was discarded in favor of directing our sales efforts to tested and true markets like Hong Kong, mainland China and Singapore. For the most part my day-to-day work consisted of writing promotional material, composing faxes and later on e-mails to customers overseas, mostly in Asia, and approving licensed products from other countries, again mostly Asian countries. It was sort of boring. But every once in a while I got to do something very, very cool.

My first chance to actually appear in a Japanese monster production came in 1994 when Tsuburaya Productions was making the pilot film for *Ultraman Neos*. This six-minute piece was meant to serve as a teaser for what was to come when the full series went into production. Like every other Ultraman show, the plot was that a big dinosaur attacks Tokyo and Ultraman Neos beats it up. With only six minutes to fill, they didn't even have to pretend to have more of a storyline than that. They got me, Nathalie, the French woman who worked for us for a couple years, and some folks from the Sales department to come down to the studio and run around in front of a big green curtain for a couple hours. Later on this was composited with some of the miniature work they'd done earlier and in the finished show I was one of a crowd of unfortunate people dodging the heavy footsteps and laser beam breath of a mutated Brontosaurus. I think I'm in a phone booth that gets stomped on at one point, though I haven't seen the film in years and my memory is a bit vague these days. It wasn't much. But in my mind, I was on my way to monster superstardom.

I continued to get little parts here and there in the company's shows, most often as a reporter or a foreign correspondent of some sort. In the film *Ultraman Zearth* I was "American News Reporter, Bradley Warner" glimpsed for about three seconds reporting on the theft of a statue of King Tutenkamen by aliens. In episode one of the *Ultraman Tiga* TV series, I'm a South American member of the super scientific team GUTS, the Global Unlimited Research Squad, reporting the sighting of a monster on Easter Island.

In episode 51 of the same TV series, I was cast as an American Blue Angel flier whose plane gets attacked by a gigantic pterodactyl type beast devastating a US city. For this they gave me a uniform and put me into a mock-up of an airplane cockpit complete with cast-off parts from real American planes. There was little more to the set than the cockpit itself. The rest would be composited in later. As I sat strapped into the seat—which was a real pilot's chair—a guy came in and taped a bunch of little plastic bags containing explosive powder to the control panel in front of me. These were explosive charges, which I was told, would be harmless. I was glad they gave me a helmet with a visor on it since they obviously intended to blow this stuff up right in my face.

They ran me through my scene a few times. I was to look up, yell, "The monster's too fast!" then scream as the explosives went off. Of course, on our budgets, they weren't about to set off any of the fireworks during the test runs. So I had no idea how big the explosions were going to be. This would be a major test of my faith in my co-workers. Each run through, the guy in charge of the explosives would shout "Bang! Bang! Bang!" to cue the camera crew when to expect the explosions. Finally, everything was set. They wanted to get this in the first take —film and firecrackers cost money. I, on the other hand, was working for free.

Everyone cleared out of the way—another boost to my confidence—and the director yelled "Action!" I shouted my line and, right on cue, a huge blast went off in front of me. The scream that came out was entirely real. I could feel the heat on my face and chest. I did not get burned, but my ears rang for the rest of the day. Later when I saw a video tape of the action, I found out that those "harmless" fireworks had created a fireball about five feet across.

In addition to acting, I also get to make up names. *Ultraman Tiga*, the show in which I got blown up, was put into preproduction when *Ultraman Neos* failed to get the needed financial backing. This show was a harder edged version of the Ultraman mythos conceived by a young staff writer named Masukazu Migita. In keeping with its gutsy theme, Migita had named his super scientific monster fighting task force G.U.T.S. He wanted the initials to stand for something in English, but had no idea what. His suggestion was Glittering Ultimate Technical Stars. When he asked me what I thought about that, I told him it sounded a little weird. I suggested Global Unlimited Task Squad.

Not long afterward I was told to come up with something for
the initials M.Y.D.O. for the scientific fighting force in *Ultraman Zearth*. I gave them Mysterious Yonder Defense Organization. Hey, they can't all be winners. And it was supposed to be a
comedy! My favorite name of all was when I came up with the
international title for the Ultraman Tiga feature film. The assistant producer literally locked me in a room and would not allow
me to leave until I had a title! I made up *Ultraman Tiga: The Final
Odyssey*. They liked that one so much they even used it for the
Japanese version.

So you may be wondering, if I went there with the dream of making Ultraman big in America and then worked at the company
for 15 years, how come Ultraman is no bigger now than he was
when I started? It's a very good question.

The answer is fairly complex. Basically, when Ultraman was first
sold to the US in the Sixties, the deal was done in a way that
Tsuburaya Productions didn't think was very fair to their interests. So when it came to licensing later shows, the company was
probably a bit over-cautious about Americans who promised
them big things.

One rumor I heard while I was there, that I was never able to
confirm, was that Saban, who produced the *Power Rangers*,
actually approached Tsuburaya first with the same idea but were
turned away. Apparently the plan was to hire Adam West to play
the role of the man who transforms into a reworked version of
Ultraman 80. Though I never found any paperwork to substanti-
ate this, it doesn't sound implausible.

Be that as it may, the 70s passed without Ultraman gaining a foot-
hold in America. And that really hurt, because that was precisely
the time it should have taken off. It wasn't until the 80s that the

company became more serious about the US market. A plan was hatched to have Hanna Barbera develop an Ultraman cartoon show. But this never got any further than a 90 minute pilot (*Ultraman: The Adventure Begins*). In 1989 a co-production with the South Australian Film Corporation did very well in syndication. But with just 13 episodes, it never gained any real traction. I've already mentioned the US co-production. The less said about that, the better.

By the 1990s, though I was there and rarin' to go. But then disaster struck. Noboru Tsuburaya died and, within just a few months a man from Thailand started faxing us to say that Noboru had granted him worldwide rights to everything Ultraman in perpetuity.

He was able to convince the courts both in Thailand and in Japan that the rights were his. Naturally Tsuburaya Productions fought these decisions. But there was little we could do. The Thai courts finally reversed their initial position and ruled in Tsuburaya's favor in 2007.

During the time of the dispute there was one ray of hope. The courts in both countries held that although the Thai company had rights to the shows Tsuburaya produced prior to 1974, they had no rights to anything we made after 1974. This left us a little bit of room to maneuver. Thus, the Ultraman Tiga TV series from 1996-97 was sold to the Fox Network in 2001.

Yes, I know. They turned it into a comedy. A grand insult! A travesty! I've heard it all. Let me tell you how that worked from the inside, though.

Tsuburaya Productions has always been very protective of Ultraman. That's why they never allowed it to be cut up Power Rangers style and turned into something else. In the post Power Rangers world, all kinds of people wanted to do that and we turned them all down. 4 Kids, the production company who revamped Ultraman Tiga and sold it to Fox, were the only ones who vowed they would treat the show with the respect and dignity its original producers felt it deserved. They had no plans to chop it up or insert American actors. They were willing to dub it into English.

This in itself was unprecedented. Sure, the original series had been dubbed, as had *Johnny Sokko*, *Space Giants*, *Spectreman* and a host of other TV shows and films. But that was decades before. Nobody had been successful with a TV show dubbed from a foreign language since the Seventies. And even those "successes" were hardly on the level you need to get a show on a major US network in a prime kid-vid time slot.

What 4Kids were proposing was very risky on their part and all of us at Tsuburaya Productions knew we had to be as cooperative as possible to have any chance at making this work. I had long discussions with Koichi Takano, who was then head of the production department, about how much leeway to give them. Takano had directed special effects for nearly all of the classic Ultraman shows and was the one person in the company's management who took the greatest interest in what 4Kids was doing.

But I was the one who was going to make the actual decisions as to what was and was not acceptable to Tsuburaya Productions. I was the only native English speaker on the staff and thus the only one who could really get a feel for what was being done to the show.

I took the job very seriously. While dubbing Ultraman Tiga into English and showing it on Saturday morning TV was miles away from my idea of the best method to break Ultraman in America, the deal was done and it was my duty to try and make it work. I had not been part of the initial negotiations with the US company. So I was coming in on the tail end. It had already been decided that 4Kids could alter the music, edit the show and make changes in the dialogue.

But no matter what they did to *Ultraman Tiga*, Tsuburaya Productions would have the right to approve or disapprove. In practical terms that meant that I, personally, would have the right to approve or disapprove what they did. I needed to act in the interests of the company and I needed to do what I thought we, as a collective, wanted, and not what I personally believed was best. Even so, in the end, communication would be pretty much solely through me on these matters. So I had to make the call myself.

4Kids clearly knew the kid-vid market in America better than I did. So I decided I would trust their judgment in most matters. And, frankly, I agreed with most of their decisions. The music in the show was suited for the Japanese market, but it often seemed wildly inappropriate to me even though I'd already spent a number of years getting used to Japanese notions of what was and was not proper background music. So I never had any qualms about their decisions in those matters. Nor was I too disturbed when they edited out some of the show's slower moving moments or even combined two episodes into one.

The dialogue was another story. I understood their belief that it was necessary to add a bit of humor to the show. I even laughed out loud at some of the jokes. But I often felt they were taking things too far. I'm not a big fan of fart jokes and I thought some of the "comical banter" they added to the show was obviously not part of the original. Even little kids would get the feeling that the dubbers were making fun of the program. And why should they take it seriously if the folks who made the show didn't? I managed to tone some of that stuff down just a little. But it took some time to get through to the folks back in America. That's why the initial episodes are far more heavy handed humor-wise than the later ones.

In the end the show never got the ratings it needed to stay on the air and it was dropped. It was amazing to me that even with several million viewers each week, the show was considered unpopular. It made me think that perhaps network TV really wasn't the place for Ultraman, at least not yet. There had to be a way to make money off a show that could attract over a million kids each week. I write books for a living these days and can only dream of getting those kinds of numbers for my work. I could retire after a year if I did! And yet it still wasn't enough for the Fox Network.

Sometimes I wonder if *Ultraman Tiga* would have been a success if I'd stuck to my guns and insisted 4Kids take a more serious approach to the show. My gut feeling is that it would have been a bit more successful, but that it still wouldn't have been enough. As evidence, the subsequent DVD release, which was treated almost too seriously, didn't sell nearly enough to become a big hit. Plans to follow up with *Ultraman Dyna* and *Ultraman Gaia* were shelved.

In 2004, Tsuburaya Productions decided they wanted to open a branch office in Los Angeles and they wanted me to run it. In spite of my reservations about the idea, I told them I'd do it. I had a strong suspicion they'd send me across the ocean without a plan and without anyone back in Japan to back me up. But I knew the time was right for this. Superhero movies were all the rage and it seemed like everyone in Hollywood was falling all over themselves to remake anything Japanese.

When I got to America I made contact with a lot of folks in the industry who were hot to get their hands on Ultraman. But Hollywood being what it is, nothing ever came of these initial contacts. Finally, in 2007 the Tsuburaya family sold the company and got out of the Ultraman business entirely. The new management wanted me to stay on. But plans for an American Ultraman film were put on hold. They asked me to return to Japan.

I thought hard about it for a long time and finally said, "No thanks." I was about to release my third book and plans were already underway for me to tour in support of it. If I returned to Japan the book would probably still sell, but not nearly as well. For me, the thought of returning to Japan seemed almost like the thought of going back to high school. Sure I could use my maturity and knowledge to my advantage and not repeat making the same mistakes over again. But I'd already been there and done that. I wanted to try something different.

I don't regret my choice. But I often wonder what it would have been like if I'd returned to Japan. Could I have influenced the new management to try and break into the US market? Could I have finally done some of the things I always wanted like put together a kick-ass re-mastered DVD for the American market (I had nothing to do with the Ultraman DVD set that was issued a few years ago, in fact neither did anyone at Tsuburaya Productions, but that's a whole other story) or get a big budget Ultraman movie off the ground? Or would I have been stuck endlessly doing approvals on minor Asian licensed merchandise and rewriting the same old promotional fliers and suchlike again and again. Of course the latter scenario is far more likely, which is why I chose to stay in the US.

My time at Tsuburaya was definitely a huge part of my life. I'll never forget the good times I had there and the deep, lasting friendships I made. I'm glad I'm doing what I'm doing now. But I'm also glad for my days working among the monsters.

AFTERWORD

This is such deeply nerdy stuff! But I love it. If I could find someone to publish a whole book by me just about Japanese monster movies, I'd do it in a heartbeat.

There are a lot of people out there who believe that if you're a Zen monk you must be interested in what they think of as Zen art. You can be into Japanese tea ceremonies, or calligraphy, raking sand, drawing big black O's on long pieces of parchment, maybe some flower arranging that kind of thing. But tell people you like Godzilla movies and they get all weirded out.

I tend to think any kind of art can be approached in a Zen fashion. Granted, certain types of art tend to evoke certain kinds of reactions that people think of as Zen. You know, feelings of serenity and inner peace and whatnot. Sometimes I wonder about that stuff. Often what's taken as "serenity" is more like clamping down a big heavy lid on top of all your non-serenity and then pretending it doesn't exist. That never really works very well.

Often other forms of art force us to face those less-desirable aspects of ourselves. By acknowledging these aspects we can then see them for what they really are. So even art that produces reactions other that the sterotypical idea of serenity can be valuable.

Anyway, I'm not into flower arranging or sand raking.

AFTERWORD TO THE BOOK

What can I say? Seventeen blasts from my past. As I said at the outset, I find some of them a little embarrassing. It's like when you're a teenager and your parents drag out the baby pictures in front of your friends. You just want to crawl off somewhere and hide till it's over.

But just because I wouldn't say some of these things the same way now, doesn't invalidate the way I said them back then. Maybe these expressions will mean more to some people than the way I say things now.

On the other hand, I feel like there's nothing really wrong in here. It's just sometimes phrased in ways that I wish I hadn't phrased it. I haven't really changed my mind about most of this stuff so much as changed the way I express it.

It almost always takes me by surprise when I offend people with my Internet rants. People don't generally seem to believe this when I tell them. But I swear on a stack of Shobogenzos that the things I think will be offensive almost always generate little or no response, while the things that get people really riled up usually just baffle me. I just don't get it.

Hopefully not too many people will hate this ebook. Because I've got plenty more of this stuff.

Thanks for reading!

ABOUT
BRAD WARNER

Brad Warner's is an ordained Zen Buddhist monk and the author of *Hardcore Zen, Sit Down and Shut Up, Zen Wrapped in Karma Dipped in Chocolate* and *Sex Sin and Zen*. He's also a featured blogger for the Suicide Girls website. In 2011 Brad starred in the indie comedy Shoplifting From American Apparel. He's the bass player for the hardcore punk rock group Zero Defex. He once worked in Tokyo and Los Angeles for the company founded by the man who created Godzilla. He has appeared in several Japanese monster movies, usually as a guy running down the street away from some radioactive mutant brontosaurus.

http://hardcorezen.blogspot.com

ABOUT COOPERATIVE PRESS

Cooperative Press was founded in 2007 by Shannon Okey, a voracious reader as well as writer and editor, who had been doing freelance acquisitions work, introducing authors with projects she believed in to editors at various publishers.

Although working with traditional publishers can be very rewarding, there are some books that fly under their radar. They're too avant-garde, or the marketing department doesn't know how to sell them, or they don't think they'll sell 50,000 copies in a year.

5,000 or 50,000. Does the book matter to that 5,000? Then it should be published.

In 2009, Cooperative Press changed its named to reflect the relationships we have developed with authors working on books. We work together to put out the best quality books we can and share in the proceeds accordingly.

Thank you for supporting independent publishers and authors.

http://www.cooperativepress.com

CPSIA information can be obtained at www.ICGtesting.com
Printed in the USA
LVOW050347250413

330882LV00001B/150/P